DATE DUE

FEB 2 2010			

THE
DAYWATCHERS

THE DAYWATCHERS

WRITTEN AND ILLUSTRATED
BY PETER PARNALL

MACMILLAN PUBLISHING COMPANY
NEW YORK
COLLIER MACMILLAN PUBLISHERS
LONDON

Macmillan Publishing Company
866 Third Avenue, New York, N.Y. 10022
Collier Macmillan Canada, Inc.
Printed in the United States of America

10 9 8 7 6 5 4 3 2 1

Library of Congress Cataloging in Publication Data
Parnall, Peter.
    The daywatchers.

    Summary: Discusses American birds of prey, such as eagle,
hawk, osprey, and falcon, giving technical information as well
as anecdotes of the author's experience with them.

    1. Birds of prey—Juvenile literature. [1. Birds of
prey] I. Title. II. Title: Day watchers.
QL696.F3P35 1984   598′.91   84-5764
ISBN 0–02–770190–5

TO MY PARENTS

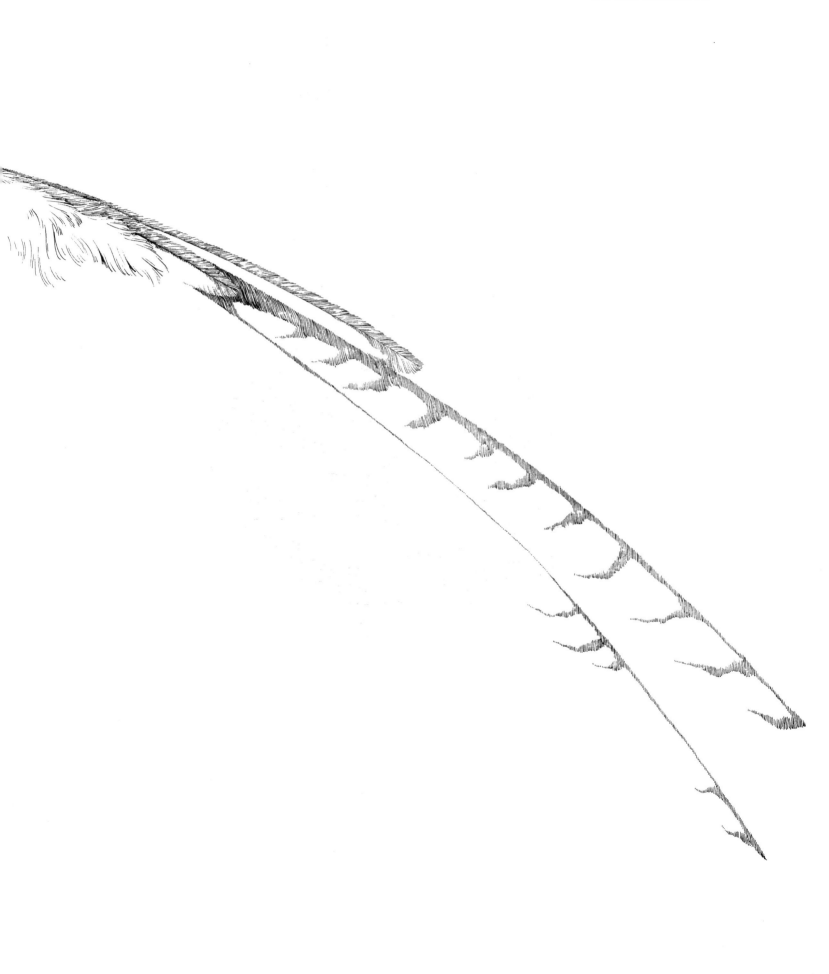

CONTENTS

INTRODUCTION

I was introduced to the birds of prey by the Craighead brothers. I wish it had been a personal introduction, but it was through a story they had written for *National Geographic* in 1937. They were teenagers at the time, as was I ten years later when I discovered the magazine in our attic. The article concerned the boys' interest in falconry, that soaring, royal sport invented by those whose hearts rebelled against an earthbound existence. It described the endless search for nests, the precarious climbs, and the patience required to train these most special birds—patience of a kind almost approaching religion. The many photographs illustrating the story reinforced my already real involvement in the boys' adventures. It was exciting to accompany them on their collecting trips, climbing the cliffs and towering trees. The nests of the birds of prey were not in the crotch of a low shade tree squatting domestically in a side yard, but hung high in impossible places; in trembling and slippery places; in sixty-foot oaks dripping with the vines of grape and poison ivy; or deep in the crevice of a cliff too crumbly for anything but a rope descent. From my mind's perch high in the canopy of leaves, nothing that moved on the forest floor escaped my eye. A squirrel searched hopefully for an overlooked winter cache. Leaves scraped quietly as an old mole journeyed under his humus quilt, intent on his path to wherever.

Huddled in the crotch of a giant tree, I began to look upon other inhabitants of this scene with more understanding—understanding that allowed a kinship with those below. They were part of the system that changes the feeder into the "feedee" swiftly and without remorse. I wondered. I wondered how many grubs, worms, or newts lay under that rotten log on the ground, by that bunch of ferns. Brother coon and I would wait until dark, then expose them and gorge ourselves royally. Brother coon. Brother deer. Brother owl. These became my reality.

Some years later I was in the woods on one of my medicinal strolls, just looking for what happened to be there. It never mattered. Deer and lichens shared equal billing. A quiet walk. A stalking, hesitant walk. Move and wait. I waited and watched, then a flicker high overhead! Movement: the blessing and curse of the predatory world. A Cooper's hawk tried to slip secretly off her nest, half-hidden by tangles of honeysuckle vines. I remembered. The Craigheads mentioned that silent exit. To the less aware and the clumsy walker there would exist no nest at all. The hawk would have flown sooner, thus hiding her home from the casual eye. My heart pounded as it had in school during the inquisition of an oral exam—painful. Painful with the surging heat of expectation. There were young in that nest, and I wanted one. From the nest's perimeter the rest of the

world blurred. The only clarity of life at that moment existed in a pile of brown and gray sticks and their downy contents. I envisioned a fierce gray bird sitting hooded and plumed on my outstretched gauntlet. A winged demon equal to whatever hunting task I presented. Vicious, raw power. And I wanted it!

I can look back now on that scene and the dozens that have occurred since with a little more objectivity. I have had many owls and hawks, have known the hardships of owning such birds and the sadness of their eventual loss. The possessive stage is over, I think. Now I want to see them fly free, for no jessed hunting bird ever flew with the grace of a wild, courting falcon! I often wondered if I

simply wanted to associate myself with these fierce and efficient creatures, or if it was the possession and control of such perfection that drove me up those treacherous trees. I know now that possession was closer to the truth. That was hard to admit.

In the literal sense of the word "naturalist" I qualify. But an expert I am not. Nor do I have a very scientific attitude toward nature, I'm afraid. I tend to classify the sharks, cats, owls, and hawks as all part of the same family. To me they are the premier examples of efficient animal life. Ants and bees really hold that title, I suppose, but my blood has never raced in anticipation of watching an anthill.

My nature education is informal. I've walked and stalked considerable territory and

10

seen unusual animal behavior—behavior I have yet to find in a book. If I see an animal do something contrary to the scientifically journaled history of the species, I tuck it away. More scholarly types have argued almost to the point of calling me a teller of tall tales when I've mentioned some animal's curious act. Sometimes I come up with what I consider a gem of a tale, and it's shrugged off as being common knowledge. But then, I have a lot more walking to do.

In these chapters I do not include many of the facts and details ordinarily found in bird books. Many of them do not interest me. I include some that might interest you in the data list at the end of the book. Most of my bird experiences have been 90 percent search and 10 percent bird; as when I wade two miles of stream in quest of a few eight-inch trout, the overall enjoyment of the outing is the reward. Happily, on occasion, the fish or bird puts the icing on the cake.

I do not attempt to write about every hawk in this country, for there are many I have not experienced. One I have not seen in the wild I had to include simply because its elegance demanded it. I've not seen them, but I do feel them. My pictures are an attempt at portraying this feeling—not every feather, but the character, the aura, of the creatures, whatever those qualities are that set them apart from the chicken and the mole.

Children dream as lions and eagles.

I still do.

HAWK MORPHOLOGY

Since men first observed birds flying, we have been in awe of their abilities. We have marveled and tried to understand and duplicate the magic of flight. Scientists and dreamers, through their exhaustive investigations, have succeeded only in discovering what a remarkable group Aves really is.

Birds have many specialties: they soar, hover, walk, hop, run, use tools, and burrow; they eat flesh, nectar, seeds, and grasses; and some cannot fly. Even in the small group of Falconiformes there are many variations.

We don't know which came first, a woods hawk developing a long tail through necessity in maneuvering, or a long-tailed hawk moving into the woods after finding success in outmaneuvering prey in a more confined atmosphere. At any rate, the superior maneuverability of the accipiters has served them to great advantage in the woods and thickets that are their habitat. The short, rounded wings of the Cooper's hawk, sharp-shinned hawk, and goshawk permit them bursts of speed and quickness of movement

12

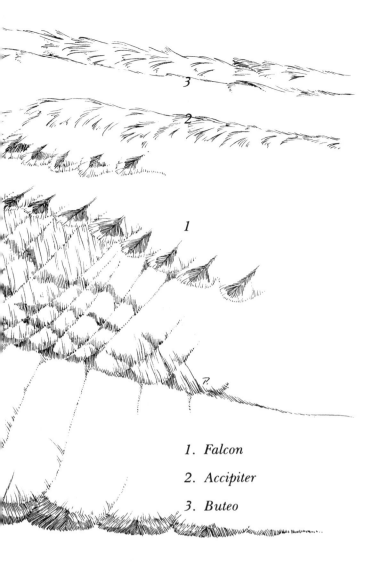

1. *Falcon*
2. *Accipiter*
3. *Buteo*

denied other hawks. Their long tails complement this ability with a larger rudder area, allowing quick turns at a great speed, making them truly unequaled in maneuverability. Couple this deft flying ability with the most vicious personality in hawkdom, and you have an efficient piece of woods machinery. Cover provided by tree trunks and foliage permits these birds to stalk their prey unseen, and by a last dashing effort, secure their unsuspecting meal.

The wings of the buteos are broad and constructed for soaring. They permit a larger land area to be covered with less effort. Though they can fly rapidly, the buteos generally begin pursuing their prey from a greater distance than the accipiters. They hunt in more open areas, and consequently they have more time for the chase before their prey is able to escape. They may hunt from the air or from a well-located perch.

I once saw a red-tailed hawk sit for several hours surveying one of my fields, waiting for a woodchuck to emerge from a den about fifty yards away from where he sat. Feathers ruffled, head sunk into his breast, he sat and waited. When a baby chuck tentatively popped its head to see if the coast was clear, the bird stiffened, all feathers smoothed close to its body. As the woodchuck slowly emerged, crawling upon its gravelly mound, the hawk tilted forward, poised. It wasn't until the animal ambled off into the grasses to feed that the hawk launched forth with three heavy wing beats, then glided swiftly down upon the unsuspecting creature. But a shadow foiled that effort! Just as the bird passed the mound, the chuck was aware of movement behind him and hunched down into the grass. The big bird tried to adjust, but his momentum was too much for his physical ability and he soared out over the valley to try his luck elsewhere. A goshawk probably wouldn't have missed!

The buteos have another advantage in soaring besides the broader wing. They have variations of spacing, called slots, between their primary feathers. The air rushing through these spaces creates a turbulence that in turn produces greater pressure under the wing, and consequently more lift and the ability to stay aloft with minimum effort. Their tails spread wide during flight, again aiding lift. Though all Falconiformes can soar to some degree, the largest of them—the eagles, osprey, red-tail—tend to do so with less flapping of wings, relying more on warm updrafts to do their work for them.

The falcon wing—long, slim, and tapered—is constructed for a minimum of turbulence and extremely rapid flapping. It is very tightly feathered and permits the birds of this group to hover, either high in the sky before "stooping" at a bird, or just above ground while searching for rodents. It is a common sight to see sparrow hawks hovering over a field when a conveniently located perch is not available. Ospreys, too, will hover while trying to locate fish, or when delivering their catch to the nest.

When diving, the falcon exceeds any bird in speed. Some experts say it can fly in excess of two hundred miles an hour. Its wings, when folded, contribute to this "missile" 's efficiency. Should other birds have this capability, they would possibly suffocate, for the falcons have a complex nostril structure that breaks up the flow of air as it enters. There is a raised ring of tissue around the nostril that initiates the disturbance. Then there is a central rod within the aperture itself, followed by fins that tumble the air, lessening its force so the bird can exhale against the great pressure trying to enter its lungs (see illustration). They say the less complicated the bird's nostril structure, the slower the bird.

Beaks vary greatly among these birds. The eagles have long, heavy ones; the falcons' beaks are short and are equipped with an extra "tooth" on each side toward the bow; and the Everglades kites possess elongated

14

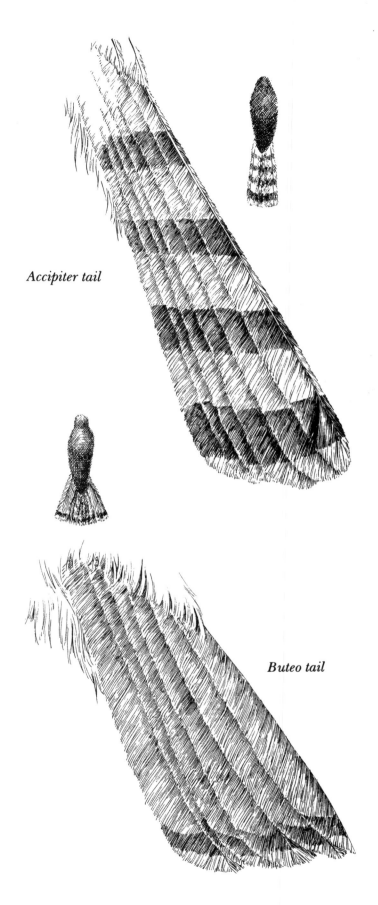

Accipiter tail

Buteo tail

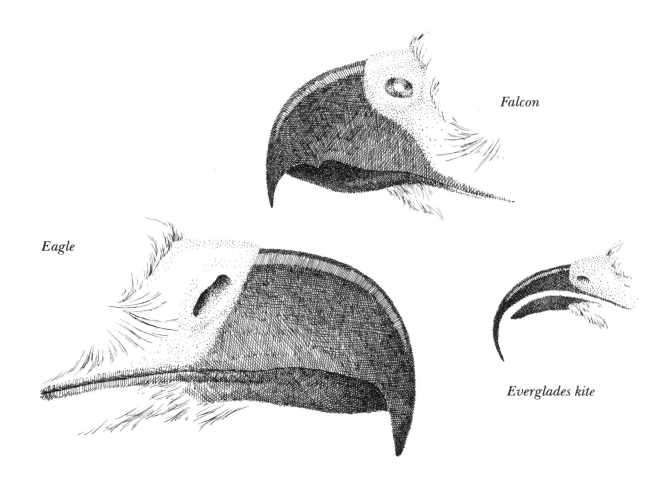

Falcon

Eagle

Everglades kite

hooks. There seems to be no information establishing the purpose for the different shapes. Kites eat snails, and it is said the long beak aids in drawing forth the snail's body from its shell. I'm sure a sparrow hawk would do as well with a beak shaped like the eagle's and vice versa! The toothed notch of the falcon gives it a little extra snipping edge, but unnecessary, I think.

That last sentence caused a young biologist friend of mine named Jim Sailer to catch his breath. "Unnecessary?" he said. "But they use that little side tooth to help them get through the prey's backbone!" Well, okay. But if they didn't have it, their prey species might change a hair, and who knows, they might enjoy that change. I had an Airedale once, named Luke. Quite a hunter in his prime, he had a distinct appetite for variety. Kibbled foods were a daily staple, but woodchucks were dessert. When visiting Loud's Island, Maine, for the first time, he developed a definite partiality for the periwinkle. He'd eat 'em in the same way kids eat grapes: Fill your mouth till you have to hold your lips tightly closed with your fingers, then squoosh 'em all at once. Luke the dog did that with periwinkles. And raspberries. Maybe falcons could, too, if they didn't have that little tooth. Maybe.

The other tools of their trade, the legs and feet, do vary among the hawks. I have read

15

that the legs of the broad-winged soaring birds are shorter than the accipiters, though I don't know why—perhaps they are easier to tuck up. I haven't noticed a difference myself. The marsh hawk has very long legs, perhaps the better to walk around marshes with! I have read, too, that mammal eaters have heavier feet than bird eaters (in proportion to body size). But the delicate marsh hawks are predominantly mammal eaters, and they have very slim feet, so how accurate that assumption is I don't know. From the point of view of a mouse or a grasshopper, all hawks have heavy feet!

A great difference exists between the osprey and his hawk cousins. The osprey has very long, rounded talons—fishhooks for fair! The bottoms of his feet are covered with sharp, spiny scales called *spicules,* which enable him to grip a slippery fish securely. This adaptation has more than once proven the osprey's undoing, however, for on occasion this bird is unable to rise above the waves with its prey, succumbing to the great weight of the fish and being pulled under to its death. Usually this bird's prey is of a small size, but now and then eyes are a bit larger than stomachs.

The Falconiformes eye is extremely large in proportion to the bird's size, and in addition it has many times the number of nerve cells as a man's eye. This permits extreme clarity of detail regardless of distance from prey. Hawks and eagles have a path of binocular vision similar to the owl's, but narrower of field. Unlike the owl, they have a wide angle of monocular vision as well, permitting them to see a wide area without turning their heads.

The practical difference between owl and hawk vision can be easily demonstrated. Find a hawk and an owl sitting side by side on a low branch, and sneak up behind them making no sound whatsoever. The hawk will fly away, the owl won't. Put salt on his tail, walk around front, and introduce yourself.

THE DAYWATCHERS AND MAN

When the first man walked our earth, no matter how advanced or primitive his form may have been, he had to be aware of his surroundings. Part of his world consisted of creatures of every description—creatures that had evolved before him, had established themselves, and in many ways were by far his superior. Regardless of how advanced his brain became in succeeding years, man was limited in his physical abilities. As time passed his creativity increased, allowing him to tie his basic rock tool onto a stick. This permitted greater leverage for thunking skulls. He learned to clothe and shelter himself against threatening weather, learned to bridge gaps in the land, and to organize for protection and a stable community. He learned to swim like the fish (though not as well), and developed physically to adjust to the climate conditions around him. In the far north his life-style and eating habits were attuned to the severe weather. Large amounts of fats and their accompanying calories were ingested and retained, giving protection against the cold. In hot, dry climates slim peoples developed who could withstand the lack of abundant water and survive on low-fat vegetable diets. Had humans inhabited deserts as long as the kangaroo rat, they might need no liquids other than those provided in the dry vegetable matters consumed. There are dark people, light people, hairy and hairless, men who can run swift animals to exhaustion, some stronger than all but the largest mammals—but as yet, none can fly.

From his beginnings man was aware of birds. The dominant images made by cave dwellers in Europe were of animals used for food, but the eagle and the owl are represented as well. Primitive societies used birds for many purposes. The first to domesticate them were the southeast Asians, who secured meat and eggs from the jungle fowl. Wherever brightly hued birds existed, they were exploited for the decorative value of their feathers. The Indians of Central America kept desirable birds in captivity, thus ensuring a ready supply of materials. South Sea dwellers killed their sources and devel-

oped a money system consisting of lengths of rope made from colorful feathers. The many varieties of finches and parrots have always been used as pets, and owls, crows, and ravens have been associated with myth and superstition since recorded time.

The birds most admired through the ages, however, were the hawks and great eagles. It was this group around whom the most legends developed and flourished. The efficiency, strength, and lordliness of these birds commanded respect, and in some cases, fear. As are the cats on land and the sharks in the sea, these birds are the masters of their element. Seemingly indomitable, they have been held in awe since the beginning.

Hawks were part of early American life in many ways. Indians of South America recognized the deft maneuverability of the Cooper's hawk and so used its feathers to aid the flight of their arrows. The hawk and eagle appeared frequently in the Inca and Aztec sculptures, ceremonial objects, and decorations. The sky, the sun, and the hawk or eagle were natural companions in the lives of people whose spiritual direction was toward light, power, speed, and courage.

The Indians of our Southwest cultivated similar beliefs to those of their southern brethren. I was illustrating a book recently requiring research into the costumes and decorations of these various tribes and found them amazingly similar. The pueblo groups also keep captive birds to provide needed feathers for utility or religion.

The concept of a thunder god was widespread, too. In areas where the condor was the dominant bird, it became the symbol of thunder, but more commonly the eagle was used because of its wider range. Thunder was probably the most powerful natural phenomenon ever confronted by an Indian, and he related it to the most powerful bird in his world, the eagle. From the far northwest, to the east coast and southward, the thunderbird became the dominant symbol of religion and war. To some he was the originator, or the Great Spirit. To others he was the war spirit, the protecting spirit, and the rain spirit. Images of the thunderbird and hawk were

used on war shields to ward off the blows of an enemy, and eagle feathers were universally awarded for acts of heroism, to be worn as badges of honor.

In Egypt the thunderbird existed as well, in the form of Horus, the ultimate power. This god was a combination of falcon and sun. Kings of the area were closely associated with falcons and the sun, for all three symbolized the "highest." The hieroglyphic symbol for king was sometimes the form of a falcon. As successive generations of kings came to power they changed their conception of the ultimate deity, and whether it became Horus or the sun, or a combination of the two, the kings associated themselves closely with this "highest authority." At one point one of the kings proclaimed he himself was the son of the sun, and therefore was

the sun. For a while things got a little mixed up.

For the Greeks the eagle sat by the throne of the god Zeus, and the punishment befitting an errant god was to be tortured by the tearing beak of this savage bird.

Always used as a symbol of strength, the eagle appeared on the standards of the Romans, Russians, and Austrians. It represented and bolstered their feelings of superiority. On our national seal we have the bald eagle. Ben Franklin thought the native turkey to be a more fitting and straightforward creature, since the eagle resorts to scavenging when pickings get slim. But historical precedent won out.

Man's admiration for birds of prey has had a more practical side than its appearance in myth and religion, and this was the training

23

and use of the birds as hunting companions—falcons. The practice started several thousand years before Christ in Asia, then moved to the Middle East, where falcons were used to harass antelope and other game while the distracted prey fell to packs of hounds. These methods moved through Europe with the Romans and arrived in England by the seventh century.

During many hundreds of years of development a social structure evolved in connection with the hunt. The finest of the hunting birds were reserved for the elite—the nobles and kings—while the lesser birds were relegated to lesser ranks. Eagles were hunted by emperors, gyrfalcons by kings, peregrines by princes and other nobility. Women hunted merlins (pigeon hawks), priests had small accipiters, children and common folk were permitted the kestrel.

In the beginning the provision of food was the whole point of falconry. Falcons were a hunting tool, like the lance and bow. But as weapons were perfected falconry became outdated as a meat-gathering system and developed into a sport, with many complicated techniques and rules. Haggards, or adults caught during migration, are the more efficient birds, for they have already learned to hunt and require only training. The female of the species is preferred, for she is larger and usually more aggressive than the male. Methods of training, paraphernalia required, and the sport in general are a book in themselves, so I won't go further except to say it is an endeavor that requires extreme devotion and patience. As a necessity its days are past, but as a hobby falconry is reviving in popularity as the soaring flights and plummeting stoops thrill new generations. They see and their hearts are in the air. Thousands of years have not changed man's emotions.

THE OSPREY

Beautiful trout streams have been extolled by writers the world over. The mystery, the atmosphere, of the more famous streams and rivers are well known to the most casual sporting reader. Described are low-hanging waves of pine boughs shading dark, sheltering pools and sunlit shallows, where gravel sparkles like fiery gems. The morning mist and the giant, brooding trout lying deep beneath a brushpile are all a part of that perfect stream every dedicated fisherman aches to wade. These storied streams and rivers do exist.

I was introduced to one at the age of three. I barely recall an image of buttons, large yellow suspenders, and the autumn odor of pipe tobacco. A strong arm clamped me to my grandfather's chest, and my feet were wedged deep behind his fishing-vest but-

tons. One arm clung desperately to a heavy wader suspender. He was standing in the middle of the Platte River in northern Michigan. I remember the smell of the pine woods and the sound of the water as it rushed by. The memory blurs. It's hard to pick out details. Only the smells, tastes, and all-inclusive atmosphere remain. I smell the trees and hear them whisper yet. What must have been in my mind at the time was the thought that rivers move trees, boulders, in fact the earth itself! But in spite of the surging pull of the water around his waders I knew this river couldn't move a grandfather.

That day a predator was born. I grew to love the river. It was beautiful, exciting. Majestic blue herons stalked the shallows where darting fingerlings and watercress grew. There were kingfishers, turtles, frogs—

a whole world for a young boy. The secrets of that river world fast became my main interest—secrets about fish. Not big fish, but the seven- and eight-inchers my grandmother loved to pick up in her fingers and eat like corn on the cob. Children are meat hunters. The size of the game means little, at least it didn't to me. The numbers were more important. The surrounding natural beauty had its effect and the traditions of the dry fly were ever in the back of my mind. But above all else, I wanted *fish*.

I fast became, not a fisherman, but a fish *hunter*. I found the final sanctuaries a trout heads for after being spooked from his favorite lair. I watched men cast endlessly to shadows under a sunken log, knowing all the while the fish had long since left that shelter and was two feet under a nearby bank. There he finned lazily, waiting for civilization to pass him by. I learned that a grasshopper bounced off the bank and sucked beneath it by the current was the only food to tempt a nervous fish. I learned that a big trout lives for the night a moonstruck mouse is foolish enough to chance the river's flow. I learned of places where springs trickled into the river. Hidden mossy places. Places where fish lay cooling themselves during the heat of an August day.

These are things a predator learns. He learns from experience and success in the hunt. These are things that help one relate to those creatures who must hunt successfully to survive. I say this because the osprey is a fish hunter, too. I have seen him hunt and have often imagined myself in his place. I have often *wished* myself in his place. Unen-

cumbered by waders, rods, and creels, the big brown and white bird needs only God-given tools to secure its prey.

There was one most definite exception to that wish, however. It was during my first visit to Loud's Island, in Maine's Muscongus Bay. I am a Florida-in-August swimmer, and the mere thought of cold water on my skin makes me wither. I did jump into those frigid waters once, and it was as brief an immersion as my flailing arms and legs would allow. I didn't envy the birds having to dive into that twenty times a day!

Loud's is typical of the many islands that nestle along the Maine coast. It is solid rock, so densely covered with spruce that movement is next to impossible except along the rocky paths worn by two hundred years of fishermen's boots. An occasional field survives as the last reminder of the small farms those hardy folk broke out of the rocky ground to supplement their existence. But the fields are fast falling before the thickening tides of spruce. The one good landing on the island belongs to our friends Cecil and Elizabeth Prior. It is a tiny harbor surrounded by steep, rocky walls and further protected by the dense barricade of trees. Cecil's bait house perches high on one side, protected from ten-foot tides by many tall pilings. At low tide the structure appears deceptively fragile. During one blow the platform was swaying with the incoming swells, giving with the tide like a tree to wind. I realized then its strength was that of the giant trees whence it came. Our original idea was simply to have some peace and quiet, to see some birds, and to satisfy a craving for an

28

unlimited supply of seafood. We had those things.

The Priors have farmed and lobstered Loud's and its surrounding waters all their lives. Through them we experienced a way of life—one of wood stoves, gas lamps, and wholehearted people; one in which great individual character alone permitted survival. One in which a woman brings in the hay and hauls her share of wood. One in which a man rows the mail for miles every day through the worst that winter has to offer. One in

which cold, fog, storms, and back-breaking labor have produced a dry sense of humor second to none. We had our peace and quiet and much, much more.

Cecil met us on our arrival at the mainland harbor of Round Pond. During the trip to the island I asked him if he knew of any osprey nests in the area. They were becoming more rare, and I knew that August might be a bit late for me to find an active one.

"Ayuh, one right close t'th hahbah."

As we rounded Loud's northern tip and

29

drew close to "Little Harbor," I saw it—a jumbled mass of sticks high in a scarred old spruce. A burned and dripping marshmallow on a thoroughly inadequate twig. As the boat slowed to enter the harbor an adult osprey soared from the interior of the island, its talons clutching a small fish. The bird's appearance was met by frantic screeching from within the nest. It hovered a moment over the nest, landed, and after a few moments of jostling and bickering was off to another hunt. We landed, unloaded, settled in, and to my delight I sighted the nest about three hundred yards away and in full view of our bedroom window—a most unexpected convenience.

I spent several hours the first few days of our visit watching the tree from the rocks on our side of the harbor, hoping to see the young. The parents were both hunting, so I assumed the babies were well developed. (When nestlings are comparatively helpless the male does the hunting. The female stands guard at home and does the cutting and serving chores.) On the other hand, if they were adolescents I should have caught a glimpse of them. My perch was only slightly lower in height than the nest, and I should have seen some jostling of shoulders or at least a raised head.

Crows were constantly about. They sat in trees a few yards from the nest, apparently causing the parents no concern. The ospreys would generally approach from great heights or by following the rocky shoreline. The crows were always aware of these routes and

The following day my son Bart and I went out in our dory to look at seals. The sea was oily calm, the sun was out, and the seals in the bay were soaking in every bit of warmth they could. They picked the most uncomfortable perches, some hardly big enough to support one end, much less the whole seal! All struck a similar pose, lying on their sides or bellies with the head and hind flippers raised as high as possible. The seals held this position until the rising tide forced them to seek a new, drier outcropping. We tried to glide as close as possible, but it was difficult. I was used to having rocks and trees to aid my stalks! The seals gave each other courage. When they couldn't stand the pressure any longer, they oozed off into the water without a sound. One big male slid under our boat, close enough for his displacement to raise us several inches. I peered through the crystal-clear water as he passed underneath the dory and was impressed enough by his size not to try that maneuver again! At that point Cecil's lobster boat rounded the tip of the island and slowed to haul a trap. The puffy orange life jacket in our bow came to life, its little arms waving frantically. Cecil waved back at Bart and motioned us over.

Bart hadn't been out lobstering yet, so we moored to one of Cecil's blue and white trap buoys and climbed aboard the larger boat. Cecil had finished with that group of traps and we headed for nearby Hog Island, the Audubon sanctuary. Another series of traps lay along its eastern shore.

We raced toward Hog, Cecil's engine throbbing fit to burst. Halfway down the shoreline I spotted an osprey high in a dead stub, and as we neared he showed no sign of moving. Cecil throttled down and prepared to begin hauling. One of the traps was very close to shore, and when we neared it the bird slipped off his perch, flapping heavily to another snag a scant fifty yards away. He obviously didn't want to leave. We continued to zig-zag back and forth, Bart scrambling around the littered deck catching crabs that fell from the boarding traps, and Cecil hauling every blue and white buoy. Each time we came a bit too close the big bird changed his perch, but he always managed to stay within a hundred yards of the original one. I noticed an exposed shoal about a hundred yards offshore. The water between there and the island was quite shallow, much shallower than the surrounding area. I could even see the weed-covered bottom in some places. Ah ... the fish funneling through here would be closer to the surface and easier prey for the bird. I understood his reluctance to leave.

Cecil finished hauling, covered his bait barrels, and we roared off toward Loud's and our waiting dory. After we had made some distance I looked back, and at that moment the osprey leaped off his perch and plummeted beneath the surface of the water. He rose an instant later, spray flying from his wings, something shiny hanging beneath him. Bart and I did a lot of fishing during our stay, and if bad luck was with us we headed for that bird's shallow cut. We never failed to catch some mackerel there.

We spent a great deal of time cruising, exploring the islands in our end of the bay. We wandered the smaller islands examining the broken bits of civilization washed up on the rocky shores: net and trap buoys, oil drums, broken lobster traps, pieces of long-lost boats, and wooden constructions whose origins remained a mystery. The head-clearing smell of drying seaweed and the ever-attendant salt air were heaven to a sinus-plagued artist. We found an old gull rookery and marveled at the objects these birds considered prizes. There were bird and animal bones, bits of metal and glass, net shreds, and in one nest there lay half a lower jaw of a small seal. Offshore were groups of eider ducks too young to fly, who, on our approach, paddled frantically with wing and foot, skimming the surface like expertly skipped stones. Higher on the land were blueberries and wild raspberries, and at one point a fallen osprey nest. We saw few ospreys but did see many old nests. The islands are so heavily covered with suitable trees that they appear to be the only sites selected (see List of Hawks). Many of these nests may well be current. We will return next year and see.

The red-tailed hawk is as common a sight here in this part of New Jersey as he is over most of the United States. During any day one can be seen gliding, wheeling in thermals that rise along the length of the ridge on which we live. Sometimes accompanied by vultures seeking the same helpful currents, sometimes harassed by crows or smaller birds his presence happens to offend, the red-tailed hawk floats effortlessly, endlessly. It makes me wish hang gliders weren't so dangerous! Red-tails are so common here I often take guests for a short stroll over the farm and can guarantee them a view of this large, graceful bird. Views are so predictable it strikes me as inconsiderate should the bird not pass close enough to the sun for us to get a good view of the light passing through his rusty-hued tail.

In winter he is not so enviable a character as we see him sitting hunched over in a dead apple tree, a touch of new fallen powder frosting his shoulders. He sits for some minutes at each hunting perch, hoping for a movement somewhere below, a movement that may signal a warm, juicy dinner. More often than not that particular perch is unsuccessful, and, opening his wings to the icy breezes, he launches from the limb slowly, beating his way to a better spot down the field. There he sits, feathers fluffed to preserve precious warmth, hoping.

THE
RED-TAILED HAWK

My first experience with a red-tail was in August, on a very hot, humid afternoon. I was on my bicycle, heading for a friend's house some eight miles away. Having covered approximately half the distance, I was in the process of feeling very sorry for myself. I was thirteen years old, and this was a stupid hot day to be riding a bicycle eight miles!

Visions of swimming pools and tall glasses of ice water flashed before my eyes, and with each vision my thirst took a turn for the worse. I rode over many little trickles and drain-offs passing under the pavement, springs and streams. But the unconscious heeds the parental warning. "NO! Who know what fevers lie breeding in untested waters!" My mouth was sticky and my head ached; the only solution was by some magical occurrence to be aged by three more years, complete with learner's permit and motorized vehicle!

Concentrating on surviving the few cars that whizzed by helped steel my nerves to harsher disciplines. But no matter how stoic, heroic, or far flung from reality my mind could carry me, the truth crept through: *Much thirst! Man alive!*

Squirrels helped, startled bluejays helped. A smelly opossum squashed there in the road even helped. I dismounted and investigated, but he was a bit too ripe to skin. Not too ripe for me, but undoubtedly too ripe for my folks. I carried on. About three and a half miles to go.

I rounded a bend and crested a hill at the same moment, surprising a red-tail into startled flight. He had been surveying a field

below from a high roadside branch. I stopped as the bird glided down over the field, and watched. Once sufficient speed was attained, the big bird swooped upward on fixed wings. He gained altitude for but a moment, then faltered. Puzzled, I could only envision a Disney bird doing a double take. The bird had spotted something, and, regaining his composure, he then angled off sharply to light in a tree at the edge of the field below.

I coasted quietly down the pavement, my thirst forgotten, keeping the bird in sight all the while. I passed behind him and stopped about fifty yards beyond, giving myself a good view of the stubbly field. The bird perched at a ready angle, feathers pulled close to the body. He was watching something. I strained to notice the movement among the grasses, but saw nothing. Scat-

40

tered about the field were small blackberry growths and burdock weeds, good cover for whatever it was the bird had seen.

My eyes were riveted to the field, but within a few moments a sticky mouth began edging into my consciousness, the two forces not cooperating—then suddenly, the bird launched! Two quick beats and he was up to speed. The hawk closed rapidly, struck—and somersaulted! He went head over teakettle, ending on his feet, staring at a totally unconcerned cottontail hopping slowly away from the spot in search of a quieter place. The hawk began running like a drunken sailor, swaying from side to side, shoulders hunched, now and then flicking out a wing tip to regain lost balance. The rabbit picked up speed, but still seemed in no danger. The bird ran faster, not losing but not gaining,

and they zigged and zagged for some thirty yards. The bunny hopped, nonchalantly as rabbit gaits go, through a small stream some four inches deep. The hawk attempted to follow. Upon stepping into the water the bird jumped back as though from a bed of coals, shook his foot, and stared at the now vanishing cottontail. The hawk then slowly took to the air, flew to a perch, shook and rattled his feathers, and, I presume, undertook to forget this ridiculous incident. I didn't.

This sort of clumsy behavior is standard procedure for a young bird learning to hunt. But this was an adult. He had to be. The red tail was the only way I had of identifying the bird, and they don't attain that coloring till two years of age.

Ordinarily we think of the red-tail as a soarer. He is a buteo, of the family of wide-

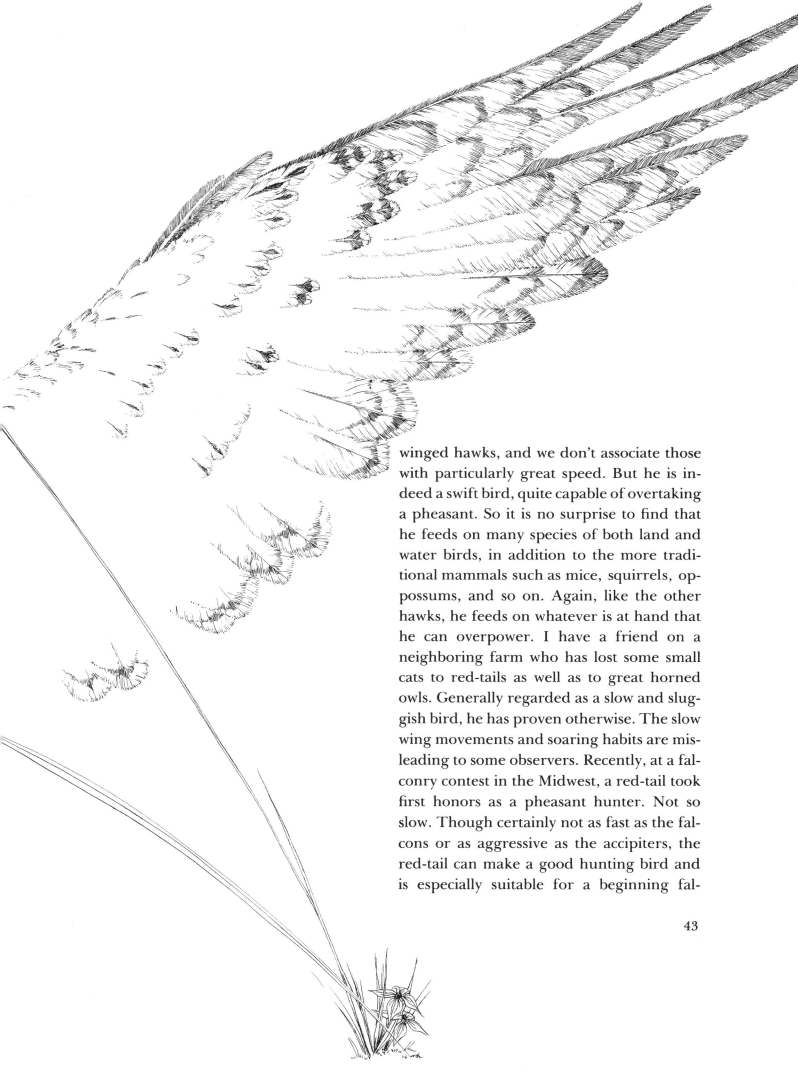

winged hawks, and we don't associate those with particularly great speed. But he is indeed a swift bird, quite capable of overtaking a pheasant. So it is no surprise to find that he feeds on many species of both land and water birds, in addition to the more traditional mammals such as mice, squirrels, oppossums, and so on. Again, like the other hawks, he feeds on whatever is at hand that he can overpower. I have a friend on a neighboring farm who has lost some small cats to red-tails as well as to great horned owls. Generally regarded as a slow and sluggish bird, he has proven otherwise. The slow wing movements and soaring habits are misleading to some observers. Recently, at a falconry contest in the Midwest, a red-tail took first honors as a pheasant hunter. Not so slow. Though certainly not as fast as the falcons or as aggressive as the accipiters, the red-tail can make a good hunting bird and is especially suitable for a beginning fal-

43

coner, as he is more docile and easier to handle than most hawks.

Hereabouts, as in most areas, this hawk builds its nest high, usually over fifty feet from the ground. It is often in a tree unlike those around it—a landmark tree, perhaps a pine in deciduous woods, or a tall oak in a spruce thicket. Like other "rules" in nature this is often contradicted; he may nest in a very ordinary tree! The red-tail may have several nests in his range, changing from year to year. A new nest is usually about two feet across, composed of a tangle of large sticks and twigs. One that has been used repeatedly and added to each time may be twice the bulk. All will be lined with softer material such as shredded bits of vines and various grasses. One I saw had some thin wood chips like those cedar chips used for horse-stall bedding. The bird must have happened upon a spot where someone had been shaving lumber and left the chips behind. They were certainly man made. One nest had some old, frazzled baling twine in it. One especially high nest I spotted about seventy-five feet up in an old white oak intrigued me. I had seen no birds nearby, but figuring it to be a red-tail nest, I screwed up my courage and made the climb. Peering cautiously over the rim of the nest I found myself eyeball to eyeball with two tiny great horned owlets! I also found a smelly mass of torn-up skunk meat, one of this owl's favorite dishes!

I went home.

THE MARSH HAWK

The words *marsh hawk* bring to my mind two distinct memories, each equally indelible and pleasant to recall.

The first memory is that of a barn loft in June. Remains of the winter's cache of straw lay like loose gold in the loft seven feet above the main floor of the barn. Here and there depressions remained where cats had curled during the cold days past. Now banty hens claimed them for nests, and eggs lay cradled, waiting to be warmed into life. The rising sun sent fingers of light probing through the worn and shrunken barn siding, fingers of light that created vertical bars of yellow against the hand-hewn beams and the ancient, dusty cobwebs that covered them. It was morning, and below the main floor, enclosed by two-hundred-year-old dry-laid stone, fussed the chickens. They greedily picked at grains spilled from sheep and horse troughs, adding to their already swollen crops. By my head a carpenter bee buzzed and chewed its way farther into a hollowed board. This sound, and those of the pigeons flapping from beam to beam, cooing their indecision over nesting sites; the occasional mewing of newborn kittens deep within the stack of hay bales; those sounds and their accompanying smells of warm animal bodies merge into an atmosphere that will never leave my mind.

47

I used to lie in that loft during some of those periods I set aside for wasting time. I've been *told* it's wasting time—those hours I've spent watching the setting sun sparkle on the iridescent necks of banty roosters and watching sparrows tiptoeing around the edge of the watering trough, trying to solve the problem of getting a drink of water when the level has fallen below their reach. What is wasting time? Watching a new clutch of chicks hatch out? Combing out the tail of an aging horse? What some people call wasting time is an essential ingredient in my mental balance.

The barn and its inhabitants are real. There is no pretense, nor are there hidden motives afraid to be bared. There is a feeling of sensible structure there. So I lie in the loft, my chin resting on the straw, looking through a hole in the wooden siding. Wasting time.

Our barn has the normal life chain of such places. The horses eat hay, oats, corn, alfalfa meal, and molasses. Many undigested seeds pass on into the yard. Oats are scratched up by the chickens, hayseeds and weed seeds produced by plants near the trough are fetched up by the myriads of little brown birds that skit and flitter about the brown ground like so many fleas. Mouse families raid spilled corn and lick a dessert of sweet molasses from the sides of the grain bins. Rats skulk within the stone foundation and its lines of drains—and cats wait. Raccoons make nightly rounds, hoping to catch a hen too foolish to roost up high. Swallows that nest on the beams of the dark stone cellar thrive on mosquitoes that hatch from water-

filled hoofprints in the soggy yard. Sparrow hawks nest high in a box under the eaves. There too, a wren has the entrance to her massive nest—a knothole. The barn and its environs breed all the bugs she could ever eat. The sheep are a neutral sort, eating, sleeping, contributing little but fertilizer for the nettles, thistles, and milkweed I have to scythe twice a year, for no one will eat them. Crows come; pigeons, doves, and skunks come. Opossums, too, and snakes, pheasants, quail, and rabbits. There is free lunch for everyone quick enough to get it without getting caught, stepped on, swatted, or eaten—a veritable nature preserve, requiring feed for only the larger animals; that is my barnyard.

From my observation post in the loft I could see downhill, past the barnyard fence, into the sheep meadow. I could also see the major part of a ten-acre field over to the right a bit, divided from the meadow by a huge stone row that traveled down the hill and into dense woods. It was along this row that most of the land-bound wild creatures made their way to the yard. Far out in the field herds of deer worked their way uphill feeding until dark, then bedded down in the tall protective grass at its crest.

As I wasted time in the loft that June morning, the sun streamed through my observation hole, warming me through. The carpenter bee hummed deep in his board—buzzes, hums, cluckings, and warmth—a drowsy memory.

Suddenly I noticed a movement out in the field. I strained closer to the hole. Far down the field a slim-winged bird floated on the

sea of grasses—a vision in slow motion, compared to most birds. A leisurely wing beat carried the bird lightly as it coursed the length of the field; then it cartwheeled! Or so it seemed. Its beats were slow, and when the bird turned, its wing tip dipped low below the grass tops, seeming to act as a pivot when changing direction. It was as graceful and buoyant a flight as a gull's on an ocean breeze. But here was no breeze. The bird hunted in an orderly fashion, criss-crossing the field, not leaving a square foot uncovered. Abruptly it checked its flight and hovered on lazy wings examining the ground five feet below. I could scarcely believe the ease with which this position was held. Ten seconds passed before the bird dropped from sight below the waving grass. I thought it would rise with its prey, but for some minutes the bird stayed on the ground, probably dining on the spot. Presently the hawk rose slowly, caught the uphill wind, and how like

a sailplane it flew! The bird gained altitude, augmented the rising draft with a wing beat or two, and headed away. The characterstic white rump was clearly visible as the bird rose over the trees and dropped out of sight in the valley below.

I had never seen a marsh hawk in our area before, never figured there were any. We have no marshes, and the open fields that would appeal to them as a nesting site were either cultivated or grazed. Oh, not so. There

was some low land down near Vera Dodd's creek. I stuck that note back in my memory, and went to sleep, a sleep directed by the low humming of the carpenter bee, fueled by the clucking hens . . . and the warm new sun.

The second memory associated with the marsh hawk is one of fish; fish and a winding meadow creek. Vera Dodd's creek. One of its sources is a small spring on our hill. As the rivulet trickles its way down into the valley and joins with other fingers of water, it becomes Phillip's creek. But when it crosses over Dodd's boundary, it is Vera's creek. At least to me. Vera and her daughter Susan are old, dear friends. When Susan was little I showed her where the trout hide and how to catch them by hand as the Indians used to do: in silence, with patience and a probing bare hand. The creek wound past the ancient stone grain mill where they lived. It used to feed a long-lost wheel that powered the mill. I always hoped Vera would be out gardening when I went by. A very cheery sort, Vera could brighten even a sunny day.

The creek winds its way through fields and around stumps, gradually feeling its way over the earth. The biggest portion of its water lies hidden far beneath dark banks. Grass and brush overhang and shade the water, providing good cover for lazily feeding trout. The largest visible pools hold perhaps a hundred gallons of water. But under the banks lie dark caverns holding many hundreds of gallons, caverns that shelter giant trout from a hostile world. Small boys fished the creek often, but small fish were their prey. They were unaware of the grandfathers that lurked below their feet, hidden from prying eyes. Nor could they have caught them had they known. But *I* knew. My own McElligot's Pool, that's what Vera's creek was. And it was a good place to waste time. Every summer rain brings a change to Vera's creek. Banks fall, brush and rocks tumble as the stream gains strength for its final plunge into the Delaware River. I fish after the storms when fish change their lairs, making the hunt a virgin experience each time. The growth there is particularly lush. Tall grass and huge willows shade the water, and cattails grow near some of the slower stretches. On a hot June day the atmosphere is cool and *I just saw that hawk!* I looked again. There it was,

up where the field rose toward the power line. It glided slowly toward me. My barn-loft hawk! Abruptly it dropped to the ground. I assumed it had caught something, but as the minutes passed this thought diminished and it gradually dawned on me that the nest was probably there. Keeping my eyes on the spot where the bird disappeared, I felt my way along the uneven ground. The tall grasses and weeds covered my progress, for they were green and fresh and made little sound against my clothes. As I neared the area I rose slowly, painfully slowly, eyes straining for a sign of movement. I knew the marsh hawk was well known for attacking intruders, and all I had on was a T-shirt, scant protection against receiving some nasty cuts. I strained higher, edging closer, as slowly as muscles would permit. Then I saw it—a female marsh hawk. Our eyes locked at the same moment as she spread her long brown wings, mantling the nest. She uttered no sound, just froze, hunched over in silence, protecting her nest and babies. I assume there was more than one; however, I saw but one peeking out from beneath its mother's wing. I saw enough. Lowering myself slowly I began backing away, retracing my steps.

As I sat on the stream bank I thought of the hawk, and what a hazard it must be to nest on the ground. This nest was a shallow affair, quite unlike the deep constructions I've seen pictures of. They build deeper over wet areas so as to raise the nest from a possible danger of flooding. Beautiful bird. But there were many raccoons here, and she needed all the luck I could wish her.

My thoughts returned to the stream. I rolled up my sleeve, lay on my stomach in the cool grass, and began feeling deep under the bank, . . . wasting time.

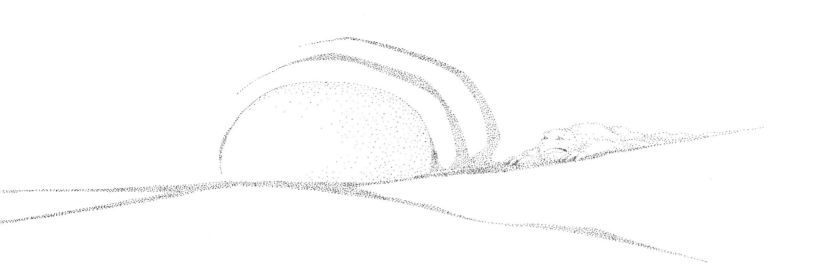

THE GYRFALCON

When I was a boy, I daydreamed. I daydreamed of knights and dragons, of treasures, jousts, fair damsels, and the great Scottish wars.

As I sat at my desk in Mrs. Lockett's class, scudding clouds high over Putnam Avenue carried me to Hannibal, who taught me to ride the mountainous elephant and master the art of war. I was with Robinson Crusoe when he discovered the footprint on his sandy beach. Together we journeyed to the great northern wastes to discover gold and avenge unjust deeds. With banners flying and gyrfalcons unhooded, we raced across the icy wastes, living on ptarmigan, hare, blubber, and blood! Crusoe, I, and sometimes Boone went whaling, exploring, and diving for pearls. We joined Lawrence and gave of our talents to throw back the oppressive Turks. Throughout the year those Putnam Avenue clouds brought Tom Mix, Geronimo, and John Paul Jones—all seeking my advice and counsel. But winter was best. Gyrfalcons, polar bears, and snowy owls filled the schoolroom with fur and feather, making it easy for me to escape unnoticed. I joined them, and with an arctic shadow upon my arm I signaled for the advance—nothing. I raised my arm again for the charge to begin—again, . . . nothing.

"Peter. Peter?" A faraway voice scraped, and the snows of Hudson's Bay began to melt as my racing horse again became a hard wood desk.

57

"Peter, I asked when the Magna Carta was signed. Now don't raise your hand again if you haven't the answer!" Mrs. Lockett would not appreciate arctic warfare. My army's overhead was low—another day would do. The heroes, the banners, my fierce white falcon, all waited frozen. All waited for the next cloud to pass over Putnam Avenue School.

I include the gyrfalcon in this book simply out of respect for its unequaled beauty. I have had no experiences with them other than to see some up at Cornell's breeding facility where they have been reproducing successfully.

In days long gone this largest of all falcons was the prized possession of kings. He lacks the speed of the peregrine, but his size, visual beauty, and his unusual perseverance on the chase made him a superb and desirable bird for the falconer. It has been observed that though he lacks the maneuverability of much of his prey, the gyrfalcon can outmuscle them in a flat-out chase. No matter how they twist and turn, his endurance eventually wins out.

The gyrfalcon is bedeviled, as are most of the predatory birds, by an occasional mischievous gull or raven. The superior maneuverability of the latter permits them to twist out of reach should the falcon turn to the offensive. Generally, predatory birds tend to flee the pesky attacks of local birds. They seem to know that a quick flight to cover is the easiest course.

Throughout its arctic range the gyrfalcon concentrates on the ptarmigan for sustenance, though other birds such as puffins, kittiwakes, and assorted shore birds are taken, as well as hares and lemmings. Where these are not readily available, then whatever creatures are in the neighborhood will do just fine.

Like the peregrine, the gyrfalcon seeks high, inaccessible eyries, returning to the same ones year after year. Unlike the peregrine, gyrfalcons do build up their nests over the years with sticks and bits of vegetation. Some witnesses have described nests as virtual cones of bones, twigs, vegetable matter, and excretions. It's a good thing they live in an icebox climate.

It was thought that the gyrfalcon habitat was far enough removed from civilization to prevent chemical damages to their systems. But not so. Our follies have drenched the earth.

John Paul Jones and Robinson Crusoe would not approve.

THE SPARROW HAWK

The cool, gray, early days of March bring a change and a feeling of expectancy here on the farm. Winter is gone, and there is a new moist smell to the earth. Fresh juices prompt dormant plants to stir, and though they are not bursting forth as yet, their time is near. An occasional biting wind or plummeting thermometer remind us of months past, but the days grow more gentle, making the land ready for new life.

First the woodcocks come. They tarry a few days on their journey home from winter grounds and make their presence known by buzzing insistently during their courtship dance. Buzz and bob, their heads and bodies up and down like feathered mechanical toys. A minute or two of this display, then they catapult into the air, rising straight up a hundred feet or so, their sharp wings whistling. After circling several times the birds signal their return to earth with a rhythmical, watery "chip—chip—chip," fluttering once again to the very same spot from which they took off! Then bob—buzz, bob—buzz. I found I could approach very close to the dancing bird if every time he took to the air I dashed closer to his display ground. I first did this at dusk in a field liberally sprinkled with cedars. I used the small trees for cover each time the woodcock began his de-

scent to earth. Three separate rushes on my part while he was involved with his aerobatics brought me to within six feet of the courting area. The hardest part of stalking is keeping your slamming heart in your mouth so the bird won't hear you! Several times I witnessed a female in attendance, seemingly much affected by her suitor's style. They must have detected me, but none ever showed the slightest inclination to flee.

After the woodcocks came another special bird. He has come between March fourteenth and March eighteenth for the last seven years. A sparrow hawk. No matter where I was, in the barn feeding animals or working in my studio, I would hear his high, sharp, returning call: "Kri, kri, kri!" Each year I hastened outside and there, on the very tip of a dead oak branch, he would be, a solitary figure clinging and swaying on a minute twig end, feathers ruffling with each passing breeze. "Kri, kri, kri!" He perched for a moment, then with a flick of wings he joined the wind and left my sight beyond the trees.

An hour later he returned. "Kri, kri, kri!" This time he sat atop a telephone pole by the corner of my barn. The breezes subsided for a moment and the bird sat quietly, surveying the barnyard. Suddenly, with a flick of his tail, he was off, only to return minutes later, calling all the while. The little male carries on like this for two weeks—waiting. He surveys his territory anew as if a new year grew a new land. Darting from place to place, swooping, soaring, climbing to dizzying heights, only to return to the telephone pole near the barn, he waits.

Years ago I put a nesting box up in the far corner of my hayloft, hoping to attract a pair of these beautiful little falcons. I sawed out part of a siding board and put the box in its place, painting it to appear like part of the barn. These hawks are the only ones that will nest in boxes, for their natural inclination is to nest in abandoned woodpecker holes or protected crannies of buildings. As it happened I placed the box that first year about the first of March. (It was an old one I had out in the apple orchard for screech owls.) A pair of hawks claimed it four weeks later. Since then the male has returned every March within the same four-day period. I always have to evict whatever starlings or squirrels have laid claim to the box before the hawk returns, and remove their voluminous additions of nesting materials. The hawk material remains the same, just a handful of rotted heartwood I took from an old stump. They never add to it, and need only enough to form a shallow dish to keep the eggs from rolling around.

When the female returns the male becomes more vocal and performs for her the typical aerobatics of the falcon tribe, the most spectacular of which is a long, graceful plummet from a great height. Just as you expect him to crash to earth he puts on the brakes and swoops upward, alighting delicately beside his mate on the telephone pole. One year a male from a nearby territory thought he would give the barn male some competition. He dove, misjudged his angle, pulled out too slowly, and smacked against the barn wall! A mortal blow.

There have been female intruders also. Because of my barn pair's fidelity (I banded them for identification), I suspect that these, like many of the hawks and eagles, mate for life. There are mortalities of course, and then one must look for a new partner. There has often been more than one female vying for the male's favors. In those instances, usually for a period of three or four days, the screeching and carrying on that takes place leaves no doubt that the resident female has a heavy hand in rousting the newcomer. The male just sits around watching the action!

Once the pair has settled down they constantly enter and leave the nest box, a difficult time for my children, for they are not allowed to play in the hay until the first eggs are laid. I'm always afraid we might alarm the birds before they are settled in! I can hear them up there endlessly reorganizing the meager contents. Never satisfied, they continue to move furniture until the first eggs are laid. There have always been five. Though I know sparrow hawks do lay more and less, I think five must be average. I have six other boxes in strategic places around my land, and though I have never looked into them, they always bring four or five young to flying age.

The first year the hawks nested here in the barn the eggs all broke during incuba-

tion, due to DDT damage, I suppose. The later clutches all hatched out. The young? Well, they just look like fuzzy little hawks, with one difference. Once they start to feather out, the blue gray on the head and wings of the males makes sex identification positive. Now and then when I open the box to check their progress, the young flop over onto their backs, presenting forty tiny, needle-sharp talons in welcome! This is the only hawk, and one of the few birds, that has male and female in distinctly different plumages right from infancy. Female hawks are distinct from their brothers in that they are much larger even as chicks. This is true in most birds of prey, but I'll be darned if I can see much difference in sparrow hawks. But then, I've never weighed them. The male is called a tiercel, the female, a falcon, and the theory is that the male is about one-third smaller than the female. I also read that every third egg is a male. At least that was the story, hence the name tiercel. It doesn't seem likely. In the larger birds of prey the size difference is unmistakable.

My birds feed primarily on mice. There are many around the barn and chicken shed, but a ten-acre field next to the barn affords good hunting, should the barn supply diminish (little chance). The only other items I ever saw a parent bring back to the nest were a tiny snake about ten inches long, and numerous bugs. No, I'll take that back. Once the male did return with a starling, or the major part of one. Sparrow hawks do feed on vast quantities of insects when mousing is not good. Crickets and grasshoppers bulk up that category.

This bird is perhaps the most visible of all hawks, and is most often seen perching on roadside telephone wires. Between here and town (about four miles), you could see half a dozen. If not on the wires they they would be hovering over a nearby field. When hunting they will often hover in one spot, wings ablur, waiting for prey to disclose itself. Should this happen, the little hawk drops instantly to the ground, pinioning the luckless creature with tiny, needle-sharp talons. One reason roadside hunting is so popular with the smaller birds of prey is that there is no cover for the venturesome mouse that tries to cross. Up north there is an added reason. The salt used on the roads during winter leaves a residue on the foliage and ground by the shoulder that attracts all manner of creatures. Even deer. Screech owls are so dedicated to hunting roads at night that they are often struck by cars when pouncing upon or eating their prey.

When the young sparrow hawks are fledged the parents begin to entice them from the nest with food. They have no opportunity to exercise their wings as birds growing in open nests do, and when their launching day comes it's "do or die." So far, all thirty babies have been "doers." For the next four weeks after leaving the nest the family hangs about, feeding, squabbling, taking longer and longer hunting forays, till finally they recede into the background of summer.

Though they generally adapt well to civilization, sparrow hawks sometimes get into trouble. One spring I received a call from my friend Bruce Wright, a fellow hawk enthusiast and operator of a huge loader in a

65

local gravel pit. Over the years he has seen animals and birds adapt and thrive in the environment of the pit. Ospreys fish there, foxes raise their pups there, hawks and owls of all descriptions hunt there—cliff swallows, kingfishers, woodchucks, herons—it's endless.

Bruce often contacts me when he has seen something of interest, and one of those calls concerned a sparrow hawk that had nested in a water tank atop a piece of derelict equipment. That in itself didn't seem unusual, except that there was only one entrance—a six-inch-long pipe rising vertically out of the top, barely large enough for the birds to squeeze in! The female laid her eggs, began incubating them, but as time wore on and the temperatures began rising toward summer levels, the incubating bird was in some straits; rather than sitting to keep the eggs warm, in effect she was sitting to keep them cool! The tank had become a veritable oven, threatening to broil both the bird and her eggs. Bruce was aware of when the eggs hatched, for both parents began flying to the hunt. At this point, when both were away, he drilled and sawed vents into the tank, one of which he made large enough for an exit,

because the babies never would have been agile enough to squeeze up through the pipe. The holes gave some relief, but even so the tank was still immensely hot, exposed as it was to the direct sunlight. Three of the young survived their ordeal, and two months after first seeing the adults enter their rusty home Bruce witnessed the babies' maiden flight.

I looked forward to reports from the gravel pit. Two weeks ago he called and said he had unearthed what seemed to be a large tusk. An elephant tusk! He carefully worked his bucket around the find, moving as much gravel as possible without disturbing the object. I notified a colleague of mine at the college where I teach part-time, and am now waiting for some news. I've been to the pit, but have never had a Wright tour, and am looking forward to that one day.

Meanwhile, winter is on its way as I write. I catch an occasional glimpse of the male barn hawk, but autumn leaves cover the ground and he will soon be gone. On a cool March day, approximately one hundred fifty-two days from now, he will return.

THE GOLDEN EAGLE

I have always been one of those amateur nature lovers blessed with a total lack of interest in technicalities. When I saw my first Stellar's jay, the sun created an iridescent blue and green waterfall over its head and shoulders. It sparkled, a jewel against a dark background of evergreens. My breath caught as this new sensation traveled the rivers of my nervous system.

That thrill was quite enough. No writing "bird #367, time of year, type of tree, location, behavior under observation, etc." No camera, no recorder. These details and equipment can mean the destruction of a dedicated "nature emotionalist" such as myself. My only concession to the proper procedure is to carry binoculars and a pocketful of Fig Newtons.

While I'm waiting for creatures to appear—a woodchuck, deer, or an early evening owl—I can rest. No lights to set up, or blinds or decoys. I have time to be distracted, to peel wild onions, count the veins of a fallen leaf, or hear the moles rustle by. There is

no deadline, and tomorrow will repeat the scene should this "sit" be unsuccessful. Hurrying from one spot to another to experience new species for record is comparable to seeing Europe in five days. An American phenomenon, I think. It's the record that counts, and not the experience. Enjoyment sneaks by too often unnoticed. Record, record . . . compete. That doesn't make a heck of a lot of sense (to me). But then, maybe lying in the warm sun, a wild onion bulb stored in your cheek, watching two ants' tug of war with a crumb of Fig Newton doesn't make much sense either.

For the professional naturalist and scientist, recording nature is a vital function. One of that category turned up early on a summer morning in Denver, Colorado, in the person of a friend of mine named Marshall Case, who, at that time, was the Connecticut Audubon director. We were both there for an Audubon convention.

The phone rang by my hotel bed.

"Morning!" it said.

"Hmmmm?"

"Hey, do you want to go up north a ways and see some birds?"

"Uh, I don't think so," I replied.

"Come on, it'd do you good to get out there and stand around in the sun for a while. There are all sorts of birds you haven't seen out here. We could rent a car and make a day of it," he said.

"Come on, Marsh. I don't want to stand around looking at a bunch of little birds flying around. Anyhow, I have to find myself a new hat." I had lost my favorite, twenty-year-old, greasy cowboy hat recently, and I really

missed the old thing. "I'm in the Great and Golden West again and I want to find meself a new hat!"

"You don't need a cowboy hat back on the Delaware River!" he replied. "You want to get eight feet away from a golden eagle nest with . . . two . . . young in it?" He let that last dribble out kind of slow.

"Uh . . . eagles?" I hesitated a moment, then asked, "Eagles? Well, uh, where is these eagles at?"

"Out on the plains northeast of here . . . a ways."

"How a ways?" I asked.

"You want to go or don't you?"

"Well, yes, I guess so. I just don't want to be doing a lot of jumping around on the way watching boids."

My wife, Ginny, and I dressed hurriedly, ate, and assembled at the curb outside our hotel. Presently, from the depths of downtown Denver, appeared Marshall, his wife, and a spanking new rental car. Green. My color. I asked Marsh if he minded if I drove, seeing as green was my favorite color, and other drivers make me nervous. He agreed. Our wives got in back, Marshall settled in the navigator's seat, and we were off. I love driving other people's new cars! It handled like grease as we oozed through city traffic. Finally boarding the proper parkway, we headed north.

The miles flicked by rapidly, but urban sprawl continued in earnest, and just as I was becoming convinced that Denver must be a hundred miles long, Marshall indicated a right-hand turn. I turned east toward what we could now see was rolling plain, and presently the road changed to gravel. Gravel roads are fun to drive on, provided there are no telephone poles or traffic. The faster you go the sluicier the footing, enabling you to play Richard Petty at moderate speeds. I began to enjoy this theatrical sensation of speed, and gravel spewed as we surfed through the countryside, raising a mile-long rooster tail of dust.

Just as I was becoming one with the machine and feeling ready for Daytona, Marshall exclaimed:

"Stop here!"

"What?"

"Let's stop here. There is a low, marshy area off to the left, and perhaps we could see some avocets."

"Avocets?" Well, as good an excuse as any to stretch our legs. We all tumbled from the car, binoculars in hand. Marshall carried a telescope the size of a bazooka, plus a tripod. The wetland was small, perhaps three acres, with some open water, many hummocky islands a foot or so across, and tall reeds along the shore. The area was just full of yellow-headed blackbirds. Beautiful. I had never seen one in the flesh before, but I didn't note "#368."

Marshall suggested we move up a small rise to our right. We did, I with my eyes to the ground looking for small cacti, lizards, snakes, and those other things you don't want to step on. Marshall, ahead with his telescope at the ready, moved on over the rise. As we overtook him he motioned for stealth. We "stealthed." Just as I began wondering why, a large, angry bird with a long, upside-down bill dive-bombed our leader. We rose a bit,

improving our vision over the crest of the hill to the pond below and saw many avocets parading about the shallows. We also saw many avocets attacking Marshall! He was busily photographing the big birds as they harassed and scolded him mightily, some swooping to within inches of his head. We never learned the reason for this behavior, but it provided a light moment, and I was bird watching. But not: "avocet, bird #369."

We returned to the car and continued to the lure of the eagles, the green machine fairly flying over the plains, dry and rolling plains, covered with scrubby growth. The ex-

panse was broken every mile or so by a watering tank with its attendant trees. The sun beat hard on sparse grasses and stunted prickly pear. Cattle sprinkled the landscape, motionless, and off to the north two cowboys jogged soundlessly through distorted waves of heat. They rode out, reaching for the West of a century past. We roared on . . . and on.

Presently another water-tank oasis appeared, this one farther off the road than the others we passed. Marshall said it was the nest location, so I slowed the car, and as we made our right turn off the road, we all craned our necks for a look at the sky. There,

far overhead, soared the large black form of an eagle. When we closed to within two hundred yards of the trees, another bird laboriously rose from the protective foliage near the tank and slowly flew to meet its mate. We stopped the car about seventy-five yards away and got out. The water tank stood apart from the small grove of trees, which were themselves surrounded by a stout fence. Here and there, beef cattle eyed us balefully from the plain just beyond. The purpose of the fence is to protect the trees from the animals, who tend to use them for back scratchers. In areas where they are not fenced

in, the constant rubbing eventually damages bark and kills the trees. No trees, no eagle nests. Evidence that at least *this* rancher cared for eagles.

Marshall pointed to the lower branches of the tree nearest us, drawing our attention from the soaring eagles, now nearly beyond our sight. There, not ten feet from the ground, rested a huge pile of sticks and flotsam. Peering over the edge was one nearly grown eaglet! He seemed in no way afraid, just curious about these creatures below his nest. There were some cattle about, one of which appeared to be a bull, so keeping the

fenced area between us I approached the trees, climbed the fence, and looked for the possibility of a clearer view into the nest. The foliage was so heavy that only climbing the nest tree afforded an unobstructed view. The less disturbance to the nest tree the better, so we satisfied ourselves with the view from the ground. Marshall took pictures.

This golden eaglet seemed a far cry from the eagles of myth and fable: eagles that carry off human babies, eagles that slaughter sheep. Indeed, this eaglet *is* different. So are his parents. The prime food source for the golden eagle over most of its range is rabbit

of varying sorts. It will take whatever small mammals are available—prairie dogs, foxes, squirrels, marmots, and even porcupines, sometimes with fatal results for the bird. Anything will do, and where an unattended fawn or lamb is sighted, it too could fall prey to this formidable bird.

In the name of "protecting their livelihood," ranchers and professional hunters kill hundreds of eagles every year. They claim that the birds' depredations constitute a major threat to their industry. Although a few lambs probably are killed by eagles, the majority of these claims are made after seeing the bird eating the carcass. In most cases the lamb died by some other cause and the eagle was simply taking advantage of a convenient chunk of meat, for it will not pass up carrion when hungry. The eagle will take birds as well, should the opportunity present itself. Pigeons, grouse, herons, even small birds will do—whatever is readily available and easiest to catch.

The golden eagle has always been judged an aggressive bird, and it is. Hence its ancient popularity as a hunting bird. Ownership was restricted to emperors and kings, as anyone of a lower caste was considered unworthy to associate with such a large and regal creature. This eagle does have the temperament to attack things much larger than itself, and there have been many reports of its attacking and killing full-size deer, coyotes, and other prey ordinarily not thought of as natural victims. I venture to say that when undertaking such odds, the eagle often comes out low man on the totem pole.

Goldens have often been linked to the kidnapping of babies. This charge seems absurd. First of all, the weight an eagle can lift is limited. Some observers say it can lift far in excess of its own weight. Some have claimed to have seen the bird flying off with loads of twenty pounds or more. I don't believe it. I had occasion several years ago to illustrate an article testing just such claims. The eagle used was a trained female. She was large, with a wing span of over seven feet, and very healthy, as her diet was scientifically organized and she was flown often. Some might argue that she couldn't be as strong as a wild bird nor as highly motivated. All right, so give wildness a two- or three-pound handicap.

In extensive tests it was found this bird could lift no more than five and a half pounds into the air—one third the bird's weight. The only possible way for it to carry off a newborn baby would be if the child was sitting at the edge of a cliff, if there was a terrific updraft along the cliff face, and the eagle swooped in from the plateau, picked up the child, and fell immediately into the draft. This would provide the lift necessary to raise the weight. Claims of lifting capacity have been highly romanticized.

The golden is aggressive, much more so than its bald cousin, but its contribution to controlling rodents and culling out the sick and faltering among its prey far outweighs any predation it may carry out on livestock.

I could only look at this inquisitive creature above my head and hope he wouldn't have the bad luck of running into some misinformed rancher or "sportsman."

My attention returned to the cattle. By now

we had a large, hairy audience, probably all wondering if our minds were addled by the heat. You just don't stand around grinning at trees unless you plan to eat them! The attendant bull turned out to be a bull indeed, though a limping one, and with the one eyeball I could see kept fixed on me, he edged over to the tank for a drink. Keeping that sturdy object between us, I crept up to the opposite side of the tank and took several close portraits of the bull, who seemed to be losing his sense of humor. Not wishing to test it further, and not wishing to keep the parent eagles away too long, we loaded the car and backed out to the gravel road. Neither one was "eagle #370."

On to the mountains. Fence posts flashed and gravel sprayed as we flew westward toward the distant mountain range. The high, snowy peaks seemed but a few miles away, for here, far removed from the Denver smog, the clear air deceives. On and on we drove.

Then . . . far ahead a post with a growth on top appeared. As we quickly closed the distance between us it became a bird, a Swainson's hawk, prey aclutch. Marshall yelled, "STOP!" I stopped, sliding some, but I stopped. The bird, aghast, toppled backward from his narrow perch, somersaulting before landing on the ground in a heap! As we piled out of the car, equipment in tow, the bird took flight. Marsh set up his giant optics even as his feet hit the ground, and reported the bird to be sitting on a post about four hundred yards to our stern, finishing his meal of rodent. But the experience was too much for him, for by the time my heart quieted enough to still his image in my glasses, he was on the wing toward calmer climes. Couldn't blame him. A rude interruption.

Now if I had labeled that bird "#371," I wouldn't have had to spend three dollars on a long-distance call, two years after the fact, to ask Marshall:

"What was that darn fence-post hawk we saw out in Colorado that year?"

THE COOPER'S HAWK

This is the hawk that has contributed most to farmers' antagonism and is also called the "chicken hawk." The result is that many farmers have killed other hawks indiscriminately in defense of their poultry yards.

The Cooper's hawk is a bold, clever hunter, and the presence of man deters it not. There are many records of its raiding barnyards, totally oblivious to the dangers involved. There are also many accounts of its ability at hunting its prey. Concealing its approach behind barns, rows of bushes, and stone walls, this hawk often stalks its quarry. Its stealth is climaxed by a final dash, its long tail steering it over or around obstacles and upon its hapless victim.

Late one spring I discovered a Cooper's nest on a hill near our farm. It was high in an oak tree festooned with poison ivy. The hawk had taken a fancy to an old red-tail nest and had done a little remodeling with a few new sticks and some bark chips. When it suited her, the eggs were laid—five of them. I happened along soon after, saw that big long tail sticking out over the south side, and figured that in about three weeks, when those little buggers hatched, my banty hens would be in for some trouble.

I was right. It wasn't too long before I became aware of a tourist near my barnyard. Each morning I went to feed: three-quarters of a measure for you, half for you, a whole for old grandfather horse, six ears of corn for the ram, and the banties stole whatever was dropped on the stall floors. I went out into the barnyard for buckets of water and—flick, flick—out of the corner of my eye, a furtive movement. Each morning it was the same routine, and the same elusive stranger darting away from its observation perch. I knew it was the hawk, but was surprised that it was so intimidated by my presence. That contradicted the books. I began counting my chickens each morning. The huge, fat laying hens seemed totally at ease—no tension there. But, then, they weigh six to twelve pounds, and not too many hawks would tussle with them if given the choice of something smaller they could carry away.

I did notice that the banty hens were keeping especially close to the barn. These timid souls, some no larger than quail, usually range far and wide by the time I am up. They take their babies to safety beyond the barnyard fence, away from stomping hooves and the ever-present rats lurking in underground drains, waiting for small victims to lose their way.

One morning I threw a handful of grain

78

out into the barnyard before I fed the animals. I often do that to treat the wild birds. Inside the barn the tiny hens hesitated, nervously clucking their indecision. They hovered about their babies, trying to ignore the kernels glowing gold on the ground beyond the darkness of the barn. Muttering, and with reluctant step, two ventured as far as the door sill, looked about the yard, and hurriedly ushered their charges back to safety.

After some moments one hen's resolve finally broke. She ran out of the door with her chicks tumbling after, a bobbing rivulet of fluff streaming across the moist, uneven barnyard. She barely reached the corn when from around the corner of the barn burst our shadow. The bird flew at incredible speed and was upon the hen before instinct gave her a chance to know the danger.

Before she died she gave one commanding squawk. The chicks simply vanished. I recovered from my surprise, rushed out the door in an attempt at frightening off the hawk, but was too late. She bore off the limp little body, her laboring wing beats carrying her over the fence, across the sheep meadow, and into the woods as fast as I write it.

It all happened so swiftly. A flash and a dash, and gone.

The chicks were nowhere in sight. I got down on my hands and knees and looked the mucky ground over carefully. I knew there were over a dozen chicks here—somewhere. They had been warned and they had hidden. How they had hidden! Two were in a sheep hoofprint four inches deep in the soft mud; one under a soggy tulip poplar leaf that fell the autumn before; two were under a flat rock dislodged by a passing hoof; two were in a deep horse hoofprint; one was in the end of the hose that lies on the ground between trough fillings! Seven more were huddled under crushed nettles just past where the corn lay. At their mother's signal the chicks had scattered like dust. Scattered and survived.

For some weeks after the attack I kept these chicks and all their cousins penned up. The hawk returned less and less frequently, discouraged by the lack of victims, and after six weeks I never saw her there again. I continued to observe her nest, however, and she returned regularly with pigeons for her brood. I inquired around and found she was raiding two farms in the valley and the farmers were happy to see the resident pigeon population rapidly declining.

The Cooper's method of hunting and its explosive attack more often than not make defense an impossibility. Like a low-flying fighter eluding radar, it dashes through woods and brush with apparent immunity, dodging and twisting, yet maintaining a remarkable speed. Its relatively short wings are those of a sprinter, and there are few among its quarry who are blessed with the safety of that kind of acceleration. Perhaps a super grouse.

As it possesses such superior hunting credentials, I would expect to find the Cooper's population rising. But they remain few, or elusive, at least where I live.

THE
PEREGRINE
FALCON

Living in New York City can be a frustrating experience for a nature lover who spent many of his formative years in places such as deserts. In my youth I did my roaming on horseback. There were no cares about stepping on the grass, no worries of bodily harm from other persons, no granite boundaries rising above the earth, cutting it into logical squares. The sky was there, the land was there, and you drank in all that lay between with no fears or reservations.

The city meant living in boxed towers, office by day and apartment by night; tunneling between through subway tubes filthy with sweating humanity. Winter was the pleasant season. Sporadic snowfall covered a multitude of litter, and heavy clothing guaranteed you didn't stick to your neighbor in a crowded subway car. Gloves separated you from the hanging strap and its thousand greasy fingerprints. Sealed, air-conditioned rooms were the only source of a clean breath of air, and if you wanted good water you could always go to your local deli and buy a bottle. Gray, sooty, smelly, confined, noisy—lovely place for a country boy! I used to take shallow breaths in the subway, hoping to reduce the number of diseases entering my body.

Plants, grass, and trees that grew in isolated parks were faithful reminders that a real world existed beyond our borders. A finger of one of these parks lay between the subway stop and my apartment, and that three-minute walk twice a day played an important part in my life. The grass, sumac, barberry bushes, and weeds that grew there were a soft tonic, a poultice for raw nerves and morbid thoughts. Sparrows were there, accompanied by the not infrequently escaped parakeet, chirping a common language and sharing their fare. Squirrels chattered in the daytime, muggers chattered at night, lying in wait for foolish souls to venture off the lighted path. It was an oasis in time, that short walk. A three-minute sonata amid the cacophony of city noises.

Whether they be from a desert or from Brooklyn, where a tree grows, city people relish their park time. It means a regular Thursday afternoon checker game for some who can only remember the good days. It means a place for a dog to roll and have a few stolen moments off the leash. It means coolness and fresher smells.

One thinks of city parks as being limited in species of wildlife—limited to squirrels, pigeons, a rare chipmunk, and various little birds. But I lived near one that had real woods, rabbits, woodchucks, pheasants, opossums, skunks, hawks, crows, and woodcock (I saw only *one* woodcock). At that time I lived with an Irish wolfhound named Finnigan, and we spent many hours in Inwood Park. Running rabbits was the favored game, but that was for early Sunday mornings before people spilled over from more manicured areas into the brush and woods that we called ours. Other days would find us in other parks for other reasons.

One Sunday, again quite early in the morning, Finnigan and I were in Central Park on our way to view an antique bitters bottle collection "down ta Fith Avinyuh." A beautiful crisp day it was. A high-pressure system had rolled in the night before, pushing out to sea the week's collection of smog, replacing it with fresh Canadian air. We had run (he trotted, I jogged) several miles by the time the rear of the Metropolitan Museum of Art hove into view through the trees. I called Finnigan in order to leash him before some lawman ticketed us for being a park hazard (I was already a scofflaw in that department). He came, I snapped, and we strode toward the environs of upper Fifth Avenue just like honest folk.

As we crossed the rear of the museum grounds, pigeons wheeled overhead, turning and twisting in their unique, daring way. A large group of birds they were. It struck me as odd—they seemed to have an extra bit of verve and dash that morning. Then I saw the reason—a hawk!

A hawk? No, *two* hawks! Two dark missiles

shot into the flock as it banked overhead. The birds veered at the attack, enveloping the intruders like an aqueous mass. The two passed through the flock, confused at not making a strike, as the pigeons quickly broke into twos and threes, each group making its own elusive trail. The hawks struck again, each singling out its own prey from among those birds loath to leave the area. One pigeon desperately tried to reach protection in the cove structure of the museum. The pursuing hawk matched its every feint, and as the frantic bird leveled out for its last few feet of approach, the larger bird struck from below, fastening tight to the breast of the luckless prey. The added weight of the pigeon made maneuvering difficult, and the hawk crashed hard against the side of the building. It flapped clumsily to regain its equilibrium, then managed to beat its way through the air to a ledge of the building. Seconds later, puffs of down and feathers appeared over the ledge as the falcon plucked its prize.

By paying attention to the successful bird, I lost touch with the flight of the other. It undoubtedly met with success as well. The action was so swift it left no spaces for thought. A few seconds—hawks, bombs— and as my wits assembled . . . PERE-GRINES! In New York City, peregrine falcons! The black helmets and long, knifelike wings were unmistakable. Falcons. Well, why not? I don't recall the flavor of the park at the time, but it must have been fall, the time of migration.

Peregrines were not uncommon in New York City in earlier years. They nested at staggering heights in the protected niches of skyscrapers and spent their days hunting pi-

timely death of one does the other seek out a new mate. The space in front of the eyrie is a courting arena for the tiercel, and on the falcon's return from winter grounds he is waiting. In the weeks to follow, the male goes through spectacular aerobatics for her benefit, hunts for her, and passes the prey to her in midair. They cavort together along the cliff face, sometimes at roaring speeds; sometimes gently touching, only to race off again for the sheer joy and exhilaration of being the fastest creatures alive.

There are sea birds, inland water birds, land birds, building birds, woods birds, bush birds, and ground birds. The peregrine is a sky bird. Its style is speed and distance. Its choice of resting sites is logical. A two-hundred-mile-an-hour bird doesn't nest under the eave of a garage or in a raspberry bush!

I mentioned there *were* nests in the city and along the Hudson—until the nineteen fifties there were. Then crept forth the ravaging effects of DDT. We now know the answer to what was then a mystery: the steady decline of nesting populations and successful broods. The answer is the same for so many of the dwindling predators: the eggs were breaking. They were breaking because of the infusion of DDT into the birds as a result of eating various prey items that had become receptacles for the chemical. Some poachers and egg collectors were to blame for reducing the peregrine's numbers in the "old days," but the main culprit is the chemical. Now that its use has dwindled, there have been experiments taking place indicating there is great hope, not only for the per-

geons, starlings, and other birds in the city parks. There were nests across the Hudson River on the Jersey Palisades as well, and on outcrops far up the river.

Peregrines seek out a high and isolated ledge on a cliff, a place that affords a long view of hunting areas below.

The falcon (the female) and the tiercel (the male) mate for life, returning to the same eyrie year after year. Only upon the un-

egrine, but for other birds of prey as well.

One of these experiments was an attempt to breed the peregrine in captivity. It was carried out by a biologist and avid falconer by the name of Heinz Meng. Faced with the realization that these prized birds were becoming increasingly rare, Dr. Meng began thinking of ways to breed them in captivity. He constructed a chamber just large enough for them to maneuver without difficulty, and installed vertical bars in windows to prevent injury. Other types of closures—screening, wire fencing, for example—held the possibility of trapping or injuring the birds. Perches and nesting and feeding ledges were installed, and when all was ready the first pair of birds was introduced. These were passage birds—birds trapped during migrations. For several years frustration built upon frustration when the eggs produced by the original and subsequent pairs remained infertile. Eyases, birds raised in captivity from nestlings, were used as well. It was found that these seemed to adapt to the situation more readily, and finally in the spring of 1971 the first four eggs hatched. Three of the four died soon after due to the parents' refusal to feed the young, so Dr. Meng handfed the fourth, a tiercel, every two hours. This bird survived.

The next clutch of eggs was incubated artificially. Soon after these eggs were removed from the nesting ledge, another clutch was laid by the same pair of birds. The artificially incubated group hatched and did well, being fed by hand. Just before the eggs under the incubating bird were due to hatch, Meng removed them, substituting some warmed pullet eggs for the peregrine to sit on. No problem. She thought they were her own. When the second group hatched in the incubator, he took one chick (and some broken eggshell) and put it on the nesting ledge. Meng retreated to the observation window, and by the time he got there the female was brooding her "newborn" chick.

This all sounds easy, I suppose, but the "putting in and taking out" was accompanied by much screaming and belligerence on the hawk's part, necessitating some padded gloves, a hat, and nimble feet on Dr. Meng's part! The young were all eventually introduced to their real parents, and their successful rearing was a milestone in the peregrine's future.

Since that time a large breeding facility has been established at Cornell University, based on the experiments initiated by Dr. Meng. Many different birds of prey have been successfully raised there, but the concentration has been on the peregrine, due to its rarity.

The program at Cornell has been so successful that young birds are now being released all over the country. Provided funds are available, the wild peregrine population should increase in the near future.

Though residual DDT is not so much of a factor here in the United States, now, the countries in South America in the falcons' winter ranges still use it as an insecticide and it remains a distinct problem.

This is a particularly sensitive bird, and the success of Dr. Meng and Dr. Cade of Cornell, and their dedicated colleagues at other universities, bodes well for the future of other endangered species.

THE SHARP-SHINNED HAWK

My first sighting of a sharp-shinned hawk came about because of a cat. I've never cared for cats really, house cats, that is. But they are superb mechanisms—the epitome of coordination. When this physical prowess is combined with a crafty and dedicated mind, the result can only be a perfect machine—a perfect *hunting* machine. I said I never cared for them because cats were simply not my cup of tea. Except for one. His name was Burl.

Burl was a huge, yellow, tiger tom. I don't know where he came from; I remember only a full-jowled, heavy-bellied miniature Siberian tiger of a cat who came down from the hills once a week just to make sure we were running things right. He toured the barns, checked out the dogs, glaring balefully at their antics and foolish attempts at reunion. Sounds of feet stomping up the side porch steps made us aware of each visit. The door was ceremoniously opened, Burl entered, and he walked solemnly from room to room, expressionless. With his inspection tour over, he returned to the kitchen, sat in the middle of the room, glanced from one human to the other, and burst into a rumbling purr. Approval, I suppose. Things were as he had left them.

Burl would stay the night, visiting, condescending to accept delicacies offered. We seemed the foolish children and he the sage.

Cats are like that. An aggravating quality. In the morning he stood patiently by the door, waiting. When it was opened he walked slowly down the steps, across the lawn to the barn, entered through the feed-room door, climbed up the ladder to the main loft floor, and disappeared through the big main doors into the woods, intent on another week of secret freedom.

This routine continued for years. One day Burl was old. It was fall. He hadn't shown up for several weeks, and we began to worry.

On a drizzly day he made an appearance at the loft door when I was up there re-stacking bales of hay the children had knocked down while constructing a new "cave." He stood at the door, waiting. I went to him and rubbed along his backbone. Pur-ring, he arched high toward the pleasure of it all. He was thin now and moved stiffly. I was trying to remember how old he was, how long he had been with us, when a movement outside caught my eye. Across the lane at the edge of the woods crouched a ragged calico cat. She waited, ill at ease, ready to flee as she watched Burl nervously while he sub-mitted to my rubbing hand.

After a minute or two Burl turned, walked over to the stranger, and together they melted into the woods. I never saw him again.

I often walked the woods to renew my sys-tem in those days, and many of those walks took me to nearby ravine where I used to watch grouse. The tangles of wild grape that grew there were irresistible to them. On one of these jaunts I did see that same calico cat. I assumed it was a female, otherwise Burl would not have put up with it. And I as-

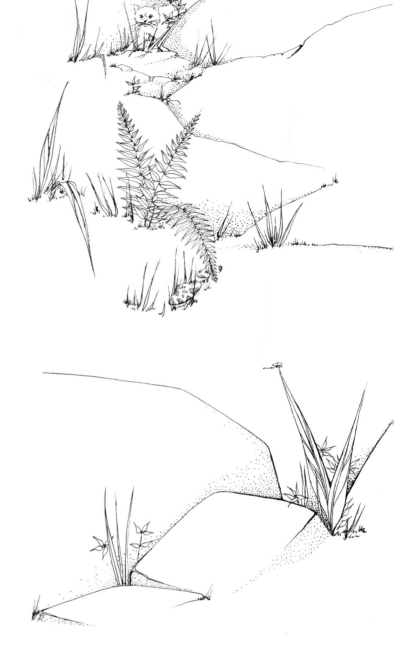

sumed she was carrying his kittens. In the days following we kept our eyes peeled and began to see her on regular forays around our barn. After each visit she would set a direct course for the ravine. Regular visits to easy mousing, regular visits to a human place normally feared and avoided? That meant kittens! Burl's kittens. And the search began.

For several days I searched the ravine and its numerous woodchuck holes for signs. Certainly they were a logical place for a cat to den up. The area is somewhat rocky, affording woodchucks and other ground-dwelling animals dens impervious to the digging efforts of the local farm dogs. There were many dens, old and new. A profusion of honeysuckle thickets, deadfalls, and a trickle of water from a small spring at the ravine's head made it a doubly safe and attractive environment. Opossums, skunks, raccoons, grouse, doves, assorted smaller hangers-on, and myriads of small birds make their homes there. Surely a good place for a cat.

On hands and knees I searched that ravine, through blackberry clumps and tangled undergrowth I crawled, carrying my trusty peeled grapevine. I probed the burrows gently, hoping to feel a hint of movement at the other end of the supple vine. Only once did my hopes rise as the probe contacted something soft. The hidden end moved slowly as a faint chir-r-r-r from a sleepy coon reached my straining ears. A sleepy coon, one grouse flushed, two toads, a garter snake, a head full of dust, and a rip in the front of my shirt were the score for this day. And the feathers . . . .

Here and there during the morning I came upon feathers. Two here, five there, mostly down and what appeared to be breast feathers, or tail coverts. Some old feathers partially covered with leaves, some recently lost. At first I thought nothing of it. I was too busy crawling through the heavy growth,

picking thorns from my skin and watching for copperheads. (I've never seen one there, but since living in Connecticut I place my hands carefully when crawling through someone else's territory!)

Now and then I found a small pile of feathers. Feathers? They were too numerous to be from an occasional chest plucking. The remains of a calico cat's evening hunt perhaps? Perhaps.

The sun rose higher, and my clothes became harbor to more dust, dry leaf fragments, thorn points, and tiny twigs, turning light cotton to the consistency of burlap and creating the winter long-john itch. Then . . . more feathers. This time a larger pile, slightly scattered. But here were wing primaries and tail feathers mixed in with the softer feathers and down. Someone besides their original

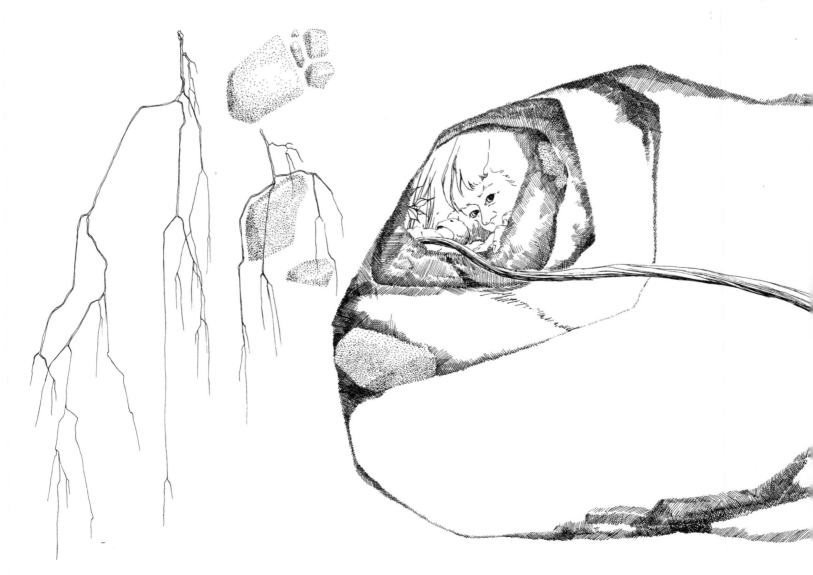

ative were the writhing, slippery eels. When such a catch was made, the gulls pressed forward. One or two took to the air, approached swiftly from the rear, and snatched the wriggly prize from the duck's grasp. Too squirmy for the gull to swallow whole without some alteration, the eel was borne back to the ice, where the bird was immediately set upon by its companions, who harassed one another with stretched wings and clacking bills, each trying to snatch a piece of the booty. Another had designs as well—the distant eagle.

Her ponderous wings flapping, the great bird was already airborne when the gull returned to the ice. The boisterous scavengers scattered, scolding and leaping to safety as the eagle landed heavily, almost losing her balance on the slippery surface. The eel was dropped, forgotten in the excitement, and the eagle tilted her head, examining the fast-freezing object. Ignoring the scolding gulls she picked it up in her bill, ran a bit to gather ground speed, and flew slowly off toward

her observation post, there to dine at her leisure. The gulls settled back to the ice spending the next few minutes noisily blaming each other for the loss. Shortly, the hardworking ducks again became the center of attention. How often the performance repeated itself I do not know. For the residents of the back coves it is a fairly common sight, I'm told.

The sight of a bird sitting high on an exposed stub during the brittle cold of winter always makes me shiver. Were I a bird, Florida would appeal at that time of year. Bald eagles for the most part are a fairly stable population. With the exception of the birds living in the far north, who do travel south a bit as winter approaches, these birds stick to their territory year round.

I once had the opportunity of spending some time with my father touring Florida by boat, and the Whitewater Bay area of the Everglades was a major part of the itinerary. Our approach was by way of Flamingo Canal, and as we motored slowly along the canal

toward the bay, the foliage and bird life began reminding me of Frederick Kent Truslow country. As the land gave way to water and mangrove growth, visual images from long ago flickered across my mind. The feeling is familiar to everyone: You know you've been here before. And indeed I had, through color photographs in the *National Geographic*, many of which were taken by Mr. Truslow.

Once we were in the bay, mangrove islands surrounded us. At all points the boundaries were the same: low, green islands seemingly growing from the water itself. Larger ones supported trees and jungle growth reminiscent of Amazon tales and poisoned arrows. Far to the northwest, too far to recognize anything but gray-green foliage and jungle growth, there rose a spire. Minutes passed, the distance closed, and as blurred color changed to leaves and stems I glanced northwest again, secretly hoping . . . and it was there! Perched on the very top of the barkless, dead tree was a bald eagle surveying its domain. A Truslow eagle. I dashed to the cabin to retrieve my camera, and after some fumbling found it stuffed in the middle of the dirty laundry bag. (It was there to protect it during rough weather.) I returned to the deck and took my first eagle picture. The camera had a normal lens, no giant telephoto, so the eagle ended up a speck on a twig. But no matter, it was still my first eagle picture and, despite its obscurity, a memorable notch. The bird sat for us till we exhausted the view and continued on our cruise. A mile farther on we glanced back and saw him sitting, still motionless, waiting for the next photographer.

Eagles will sit for hours at their favorite lookout points waiting for the right fish, the right water bird, or the right osprey carrying the right fish! On that same trip when we were near Naples, Florida, I saw the oft-described thievery take place. As we motored around a watery bend, an osprey flew into view over the mangrove tops carrying a small fish. It crossed our bow at an altitude of about two hundred feet, flying unhurriedly. Suddenly it rose abruptly, and from the island on our left a bald eagle appeared, racing on a collision course, quickly closing the gap between the two birds. Both rose rapidly as the distance lessened, and when it seemed contact was imminent the osprey collapsed, quickly losing altitude, the eagle hard on its trail. A flurry of feinting and parrying took place as both birds fell toward the water. Finally in desperation the osprey dropped its prey and escaped out of our sight over a mangrove clump. The eagle stooped for the falling fish, missed, then circled, plucked it from the surface of the water, and was gone. The whole incident took no longer than fifteen seconds.

Bald eagles sometimes manage to steal a meal this way, but more often than not they catch their fish themselves. Sometimes they take the fish from the surface—fish sunning themselves, or perhaps the sick or injured. In some areas where fish congregate in schools, eagles find hunting easy, and where salmon spawn, eagles often eat the dead and dying along the shore. Where fish are more scarce, water birds often fall prey to their powerful talons. Land birds are also on the food list. There are reports of grouse being

101

taken, and even smaller birds meet an eagle at the wrong time and unwillingly add to its calories. Somehow I can't visualize a bird that large outmaneuvering a sparrow, but that's what I've *heard*.

In the "good old days," when bald eagles could be seen a dozen at a time in the north country, a bounty was offered for them. It was primarily the result of pressure from groups of fishermen and trappers who felt that the eagles were making serious inroads on their economic stability by killing off their sources of livelihood. Thousands of eagles were slaughtered, with economics serving as the excuse, when actually no proof was ever presented to verify the bird's depredations. They preyed chiefly upon the sick and injured, those that were of no use to man by any stretch of the imagination.

Like the osprey's, the eagle's eyes are sometimes bigger than its stomach and it occasionally makes the fatal error of grabbing a fish too big to handle. The osprey hunts from a great height and literally plunges beneath the surface for its prey. The eagle, on the other hand, usually hunts from a land-based vantage point, then flies low over the water, barely wetting its legs as it plucks a fish from just beneath the surface. There are eyewitness accounts of eagles holding fast to the backs of large fish, and, unable or unwilling to let go, being dragged below the surface and drowned. One observer found a huge salmon washed onto a river bank with a drowned eagle firmly attached to its back. The eight talons were interlocked deep in the flesh, hitting no vital organs. The salmon could have lived for days, its burden slowing

it just enough to prevent feeding, until it finally starved to death.

The bald eagle has its detractors: those calling him a scavenger (which he sometimes is), a coward (which I would question), and a menace to things warm and fuzzy (aren't we all). He is without a doubt a vigorous and elegant creature. His size, beauty, and noble countenance make him an ideal symbol. I never could understand Mr. Franklin's lobbying in favor of a turkey for our national bird. My spirit doesn't soar at the thought of something plodding along the ground saying "gobble, gobble."

THE GOSHAWK

This is a bird of the northern forests, though of the three I have seen in the wild, only one was in a northern forest. That was in the White Mountains of northern New Hampshire, in the winter.

I enjoy quiet. The quietest place I know of is a winter camp as far away from civilization as I can get. A thick blanket of snow blends trees and earth together, creating a world of down and marshmallows. The real world disappears and the thick white blanket removes stalks and thorns from the mind. No rustles or snaps, only quiet. The snow muffles all sound in the cold still air, and deer pass scant yards away, unheard. Drifts hide grouse deep from creatures that prowl, and the bears are asleep in their dens beneath the snow.

The aesthetic side of winter lay spread before me as I stood gazing at a white, flat expanse that in summer is Bartlett's Pond. That is my first memory of winter at the pond.

My second memory is of my breath coming in labored gulps, the cold air threatening to freeze my totally inadequate lungs. I had just traveled two miles through deep snow with a sixty-pound pack, using unfamiliar muscles, muscles that now quivered, begging for a rest. My camp was a short way up the hill on the edge of a smaller pond, so summoning what reserve I had left, I made for it.

I had camped here many times before. The frame for my tarp tent was intact, reflector logs for my fire were there, and some thoughtful summer hiker had left two small, dead spruces propped against the tarp frame for firewood. Bless him.

Shortly, I was nicely settled in, my wet un-

dershirt was drying by the fire, and raisin oatmeal soon bubbled in my blackening pot. Except for the crackling fire, it was quiet. Winter quiet. And dark.

In the morning after breakfast I stepped out onto the windblown ice of the large Bartlett's Pond and headed for the beaver dams that slow the flow feeding the pond. There are many dams crossing one another, creating individual pools that have trapped huge brook trout. It seems like a man-made maze. The first time I saw the area it reminded me of a hatchery, with catwalks on which you could walk and examine the fish trapped below. Now it was frozen, the fish waiting under the ice, waiting for spring hatches to make them fat again.

I stood on a dam, not thinking of anything in particular, just vacantly enjoying the woods before me, when suddenly there came a sharp squeak from within the woods ahead. Quickly following it came a high-pitched baby's screech. I knew the sound. A squirrel, caught in a mortal grip. The powdery snow muffled my steps as I swung my snowshoes as best I could. When I reached the cover of a stand of firs I heard another sound, and froze. I raised my eyes slowly. Blood surged under an over-tight collar and I waited. Suddenly the bird could stand my presence no longer and he flushed forth, a surging mass of gray and white, flying low, dodging trees, gaining speed with every twist and turn, then vanished. My first wild goshawk.

I hurried to the spot where intuition said I saw him first. There on the ground was the story of a struggle, brief and to the point. Six feet from where the hawk first struck, the snow was trampled. He must have intended to carry off the prey, but it struggled or bit his foot, so he landed, to finish the kill on the spot. Two specks of red and a tuft of squirrel hair were all that remained.

To the reader this must seem like a lot of buildup for precious little hawk story, but that's how it happens. You don't run into the woods and see fourteen hours of goshawk activity!

I mentioned that the goshawk is a northern forest bird, but it's not always so. I was visiting the Connecticut Audubon center in Fairfield one summer, sitting in my friend Marshall Case's office talking about one thing or another, when a young boy floundered excitedly into the room.

"Mr. Case, there's a goshawk at the pond!"

"Are you sure, Tommy?" Marshall asked.

"Yes, yes!"

"What was it doing?" asked I.

"Killing wood ducks!" he replied breathlessly. At that Marshall straightened up a bit.

"Where?"

"Down at the *pond*!!"

The boy ran out without further explanation, and we prepared to follow. The phone rang, delaying our exit, and by the time the conversation was over Tommy returned. Marshall asked, "Was it really after the ducks?"

"Yup. There were *two* goshawks. And each killed a duck. And I took a picture of them!"

I never got to see the photographs, but I'm sure they exist.

The goshawk has frequently been described as the boldest, most vicious member of the predatory bird family. Many reports

of barnyard forays are on record, some of them taking place in the presence of the farmer himself! Humans generate little fear in the heart of this gray demon when hunger strikes.

The most recent occurrence I am familiar with concerned the local game warden, who is a farmer and keeps a few chickens for table eggs.

Like most of us he lets his flock range out of their pen during the day to cut a few hairs off his feed bill. One evening he came home from the fields, went to usher his birds into the coop, and just as he rounded the corner of his barn a large bird rushed past him. In confusion he stared, yelled "Hey!" and before he could find a rock to throw, a large goshawk sat plucking one of his fattest hens! The warden then ran at the bird, driving it away. They had chicken for dinner that night.

Two days later another dead hen was found, well plucked and partially eaten. He called me. Harold (the warden) identified the bird as a goshawk, had never seen one before, and asked me what it was doing around those parts. I told him it was killing his chickens. I also told him it could be a migration spillover, or possibly a local bird. I saw a goshawk on my farm a few weeks before. It was probably the same one.

The next day I took over a leather harness covered with dozens of nylon slip nooses attached to it. It was one I had used to snare some hawks in years past. In the afternoon Harold tied the harness on the back of one of his hens, tethered her out near the coop, and waited. He waited over four hours. Fi-

nally the hawk returned, struck at the frantic hen, and got its toes firmly entrapped in the snares. The last time I saw that red-eyed, ill-tempered bird it was being carried, firmly trussed up in an old woolen sock, to a distant point in New York. The chickens were rooting for a one-way trip.

The goshawk is probably the most aggressive and temperamental of the hawk family, followed closely by its accipiter cousins. They all look rather similar except in size—slate gray above, light and barred below, with long, heavily barred tails. Because of their aggressiveness and swift acceleration they have always been a favorite of falconers the world over. The hunting birds that are true falcons hunt from on high, sighting and stooping to their own prey. The goshawk is hunted from the fist and launched once the prey is sighted—to me by far the more personal and exciting experience.

The goshawk, like the great horned owl, had a bounty on its head in years past, for they both take considerable game. But their benefits far outweigh their drawbacks. Unfortunately any hawk is a chicken hawk to many farmers. I was in the woods one fall looking for old nests; it was the hunting season, and far down the hill I saw a man approaching with a gun. I edged carefully over the stony ground toward him, and as I neared a heavy clump of honeysuckle a large horned owl flushed forth. Taking four quick wing beats he cleared the trees and glided majestically down the hill toward the hunter.

Blam! Blam!

Then I heard a curse, and:

"Durn chicken hawk."

for the old deer's neck to have been so worn.

I returned on several occasions to confirm the lessons and the hawk's hunting technique, and saw them both repeated.

I mentioned before that these were young deer. And you may question the eight-pointer. The hunting pressure in western New Jersey is great, and rarely does a buck live past two years. We aged some deer at the local inspection station one year and found none over twenty-one months old, the average ages being between sixteen and nineteen months. Among those were many deer with six and eight points.

Broad-winged hawks are supposed to be fairly common in our area, but I haven't seen too many close up. On my spring rounds of the woods and hills I have looked for their nests, and over the years positively identified only three. These retiring birds tend to nest in more remote areas than most hawks do.

The one nest I saw in progress was a slap-dash affair, the birds being devoid of the industry usually associated with nest-building. They just hung around between hunting trips, throwing a stick on when the impulse hit them. I wondered if they were a little embarrassed by their lack of style, for they continued to remodel here and there till the chicks were ready to leave home. A new twig here, a new leaf there, like my wife deciding the kitchen curtains need changing. I have read that this reupholstery tendency is common among broad-wings. It's reassuring to have my observation verified by scientific fact.

Recently I read: "In late spring the woods are filled with the screams of mating broad-wings." Whoever wrote that must have been in the Bronx Zoo, for he never has been in *our* woods.

THE RED-SHOULDERED HAWK

The first creature totally to capture my imagination was a red-shouldered hawk. I was away at summer school (a prerequisite to this less-than-enthusiastic student's readmission in the fall), feeling left out of the world and in desperate need of something tangible to care about. One morning I was in the biology lab escaping from the worry of a forthcoming algebra exam, when a classmate burst through the door, breathless. He carried a small ball of down in his cupped hands. A baby hawk! We quickly went to several bird books, searching for whatever information was available on hawks. We couldn't tell what kind it was of course, all baby hawks are so similar. But we compared it to photos of other nestlings and guessed it to be about ten days old.

The bird had been found near the road to the gymnasium, where the pavement wound through a stand of dense woods. We went there, one white fluffy hitchhiker secure in my shirt pocket, and began the search for the nest. We looked all afternoon, intent on locating the lost baby's home (secretly hoping we wouldn't find it). Not meeting with any success, the first problem was what to do with the bird, and, "keep it, keep it!" won out. We returned to the lab and proceeded to fix up a small cage. The bird was still far too young to be kept on a flat surface, so a small bowl was located, lined with many tissues, and the little bird placed inside. Its chin rested just on the edge, and the cavity was the right size to keep the baby from falling over. We secured permission from the lab faculty director to keep the bird, and for reasons unknown declared it a female. We named her Leda. Also for no logical reason.

During the weeks that passed we fed Leda royally on excess lab mice and chicken innards, and dreamed of the day when we would ahawking go. Our horizons widened to a point where we lost all sense of reality. Heroics were performed by the two of us and our bird. And this being a boys' boarding school far from female companionship, there were always fair maids waiting in the wings of our minds for heroes to rescue.

The difficulties and time involved in caring for a bird of prey dulled my young friend's enthusiasm, however, and after a few weeks Leda was left in my care. Algebra homework took a back seat as the hawk grew strong and large on my begged and borrowed offerings. I knew nothing of the nutritional needs of such birds, only that whole animals are a balanced diet. And whole animals she got.

When the bird was about a month old and able to lurch around the ground on her own, we began to take excursions into a hayfield in back of the laboratory. The days were hot, the flies hummed, I snoozed, and Leda poked around the grasses, snapping up both bugs and clover blossoms with equal relish. She hopped and stumbled about like a wobbly foal, finding a new world to stalk and conquer behind every clump of grass.

The days passed, Leda's feathers grew long and firm, and she began taking short, frightened flights above the grasstops. She would spread her wings, flap excitedly, and move semi-airborne across the grass, looking for all the world like a feather duster on a moving trampoline. Gradually she grew more competent, her flights grew stronger, and the thought of losing her weighed heavily on my mind. I had always made a sharp whistle sound before she was fed, so even when flying she reacted to the sound and, wheeling about, returned for a little meat treat, much to my relief. Though her flights improved, she never shed the habit of walking about the ground. She became more interested in its whys and wherefores as her gait grew more graceful and her attention wasn't totally focused on remaining upright. She would take a few steps, stop and listen, much as a robin does when searching for worms. She was so persistent in this action I began to wonder about it. Since her first flight she had never caught anything on her own except for an insect now and then, but now Leda seemed

intent on a search for something. Something she knew was there.

Late one afternoon I took Leda from her cage in the lab and carried her to the far end of the hayfield. Black-eyed Susans grew in clusters there. The thistles had grown high, the grasses had begun to droop, and the smell of the height of summer was in the air. I set the bird down on a clump of grass and sat beside her. She stayed for a moment, then ambled off to her investigations. When she walked she rolled as if walking a heaving deck. Shoulders hunched and head held low she stopped, cocked her head, and listened. This time she didn't move on. Her head swayed from side to side as if zeroing in on some sight or sound. She was motionless for an instant, then, leaping ahead a step, she began tearing at the ground beneath her. Dried grass flew as Leda tore at the spot with

bill and talons. She dug frantically, then stopped, staring at the ground in front of her. I got up as she began feeding, and found she had uncovered a nest full of baby mice! She gobbled down each and every one. She seemed quite pleased with herself and chortled in the hot sun as she swallowed her first earned meal.

In the days to follow (when I could escape the classroom) we walked and hunted every field on the school farm. Successfully, I might add, though our game was confined to mice, grasshoppers, and an occasional frog. A small garter snake was an added treat one day. She swallowed it whole, and for minutes afterward her crop undulated as the still-live snake searched frantically for an exit. After that experience she was a bit more precise in her kill.

Haying time brought a new lesson for

118

Leda. By now she was fully feathered and began taking longer and longer flights. The reality of her approaching independence was dawning on me, though she still came readily to the whistle and a promise of an easy snack. Early one morning, about an hour before the breakfast bell was due to call us back to earth, we went to a recently cut field between school and the river. The hay had been baled two days before. There was no threat of rain, so the bales had been left on the ground. It was a long walk down off the school hill and Leda weighed heavily on my arm, so as we reached level ground I launched her into the air. She stretched her wings gratefully after a stuffy night in the laboratory and flew slowly over the field in a large circle. Then I whistled, calling her to my arm for a small percentage of breakfast. I gave her a tiny

piece of liver and placed her on a hay bale. I sat on another and wondered just what kind of fish waited over there in the river for a personally designed piece of Parnall bait. I also wondered what the penalty would be for missing my next class. Boys wonder, wonder about things and at things. And they wonder what difference one algebra class is going to make in ten years. I still do.

Suddenly Leda crouched on the bale and began her Siamese head dance. She looked, swayed her head from side to side, trying to zero in on something by the bale of hay. At first I thought she was practicing on a moving grass tip. Not so. Something was there. I picked her up, and once she was settled on my arm her attention returned to the bale. I kicked it over with my foot, and Leda leaped from my hand as three mice scuttled for

safety under another bale. Not having time to use her wings, she lurched after one poor soul who made an error in direction. Three bird steps and he was added to breakfast. From that point on Leda became an excellent hayfield mouser! In the days to follow she flew in small circles as her personal bale kicker performed his duty. (Some of the bales *did* get rained on and were left in the field to rot.) From this point on other game was taken from a flying approach as well.

Frogs, snakes, an occasional rabbit, all were caught with equal accuracy. Rarely now was a long search wasted by adolescent fumbling. No longer running down her prey, she hunted like a wild bird, and her self-sufficiency became evident.

Summer school's end soon drew near, as did my happy encounter with red-shoul-

dered Leda. No longer kept in a cage now, she was free to come and go and roost where she pleased, though her favorite spot was in the grove of pines near the biology lab. She still regularly hunted her school fields, and several times before I left I whistled her in when I saw her flying nearby. She came, but somewhat reluctantly. The offerings I had for her were not so alluring now. She would sit on my arm for a moment or two looking off across the drying field, then, lifting her wings on a fresh breeze she would be off. Off to her own places—places without cages, baby-sitters, and bale kickers. Almost thirty years have passed since Leda, and I can still smell those fresh-cut, mousy fields.

RED-SHOULDERED HAWK

COOPER'S HAWK

SPARROW HAWK

SHARP-SHINNED HAWK

PIGEON HAWK

PEREGRINE FALCON

HARRIS' HAWK

EVERGLADES KITE

SWAINSON'S HAWK

GOLDEN EAGLE

BALD EAGLE

MARSH HAWK

GOSHAWK

GYRFALCON

OSPREY

BROAD-WINGED HAWK ·

RED-TAILED HAWK

FERRUGINOUS ROUGH-LEGGED HAWK

PRAIRIE FALCON

LIST OF HAWKS

BALD EAGLE (*Haliaeetus leucocephalus*)

The white head and tail of our national bird make it unmistakable, whether it is perched high over the waters on a lofty snag or soaring nearly out of eyes' reach. This is the only eagle confined solely to our continent, a majestic bird in stature, perhaps less than majestic in some of its carrion-eating habits. This eagle has declined rapidly over the recent past due to pesticides ingested through its prey, making the eagles' eggs brittle and prone to breaking.

The nest of this bird can be huge. It is added to year after year, reaching depths of over ten feet. Some become so heavy they topple the supporting tree. Many different materials have been found aboard—socks, netting, corn stalks—whatever flotsam appeals is laced into the huge pile of sticks. A Doctor Francis Herrick relates in Bent's *North American Birds of Prey* that he found sticks two inches thick and six feet long in one nest he was observing. Grass, weeds, and other softer materials are used to line the nest.

The food list of the bald eagle includes many different species of fish that the bird either catches from the water or picks up on shore after they have died and been washed up. Many years ago there were large groups of eagles reported waiting for salmon and herring to finish spawning, die, and be washed ashore. These birds take rabbits, muskrats, and many different types of water birds, but the bulk of the diet is fish.

Generally two, sometimes three, young are hatched, and they reach mature coloration in four years. Their feet have spicules on the soles, common among fish catchers, aiding in the holding of slippery objects. The bald eagle is usually slightly smaller than the golden eagle, but in some cases could be of similar size.

GOLDEN EAGLE (*Aquila chrysaëtos*)

The golden eagle is the largest of our two eagles, the females attaining a length of almost three and a half feet, with a seven-foot-plus wing spread. The young gradually lose the white on the wings and tail and at about four years gain their adult plumage, rather dark brown with yellowish brown on the head and neck. The white juvenile tail feathers tipped with black were a favorite item in Indian traditions.

The golden's range is coast to coast and from northern Canada south, with the exception of the Southeast section of the country. It is also found in Asia and Europe.

This bold bird has the strength and ability to secure large game, but it generally feeds on rabbits, prairie dogs, snakes, and such. The list of prey is huge and includes any creature in the vicinity small enough for the eagle to overpower. Occasionally it will eat carrion when no fresh food is available, and like the bald eagle it is not above stealing an osprey's hardwon meal. The taking of lambs, children, and other "cuddly" creatures is highly contested and over the years has been blown out of proportion by special interests. Like all birds of prey the golden eagle benefits man and nature greatly by eliminating the weak and sick, and by cutting down the pest population.

These birds usually nest on cliff ledges where available, for the warm, rising currents make it easier for them to carry weight and to take off. In forests they will choose a tall tree. Sometimes on the plains a small tree is the only possibility and is used to the best advantage.

The nest is a large affair, constructed of big sticks, lined with smaller, softer materials, such as inner barks and grasses. There are usually two eggs, incubated by the female for over a month.

123

PEREGRINE FALCON (*Falco peregrinus*)

Found worldwide, the peregrine, or "duck hawk," has long shared an association with man. For hundreds of years it has been thought of as the epitome of the hunting bird, because of its extreme speed and spectacular stoops from great heights to its prey. Only recently have several ornithologists declared that they believe the gyrfalcon to be faster in level flight.

The adult peregrine has a black head with thick moustache stripes, is gray above, and barred. The underparts are light. The female is barred slightly more heavily than the male. She is considerably larger, at seventeen to twenty inches, some six inches longer than the male. As in most birds of prey, she is more aggressive as well.

These hawks feed primarily on birds. Ducks, pheasants, shore birds—birds of this size—form a part of the diet, but medium-size birds such as jays, pigeons, woodcocks, and small hawks are the bulk of the diet. Smaller birds are taken as well, when available. Small mammals and insects are also taken, but in small number.

The nest is usually high on a rocky ledge, with little material other than pebbles, sand, and twigs found there and scraped a bit by the bird. Three to five mottled eggs are laid in the resulting depression.

From this high vantage point the young can often see their parents approach after a successful hunt and become quite excited at the nearness of a meal! The adults put this excitement to good use as the youngsters approach flying age, and will often drop the prey in an attempt at provoking the excited young into flight. The ruse eventually works. The male will feed the incubating female in this same manner.

RED-TAILED HAWK (*Buteo jamaicensis*)

One of our largest and most recognizable hawks, the red-tail can be seen in every part of our country. Soaring, catching thermals under its broad, long wings, it surveys the countryside seemingly without effort. As it wheels and glides, its reddish-brown tail is spread wide, its color glowing as the sun passes through. It hunts from high and also from a perch in an orchard tree or on a branch at the edge of a field. It sits upright, fat and bulky, resting as comfortably as possible until its prey is sighted. If no prey appears, the hawk will launch itself from that stand, glide across the field, and gracefully arc upward into another tree. It may travel only fifty yards, and if a few wing beats are necessary, they are slow and even.

The plumage of the adult red-tail is basically brown above with the exception of the tail, light below with brown barring on the upper legs. The tail has one black band just in from a white tip. The Western red-tail tends to be darker overall. These hawks are large, with a wing span to four and one-half feet.

The nest is generally high in a hardwood tree, built in a crotch forty to sixty feet from the ground. Or, where no trees are available, nests are built on ledges or in tall saguaro cacti. Old nests of other large hawks may be redecorated and used, but more often the red-tail constructs his own out of large twigs, lining it with inner barks and garnishing it with a few evergreen sprigs. They are wide, up to twenty inches, and though of varying depths, have a shallow depression up to six inches deep to hold the eggs, of which there are usually two or three. The nest is often used year after year. But just as often the pair will have several nests, returning to each after several years' absence. The red-tail is not a nest protector, for it steals off at the first sign of intrusion, returning only after the coast is clear.

COOPER'S HAWK (*Accipiter cooperii*)

This is the "villain" that caused the term *chicken hawk* to be coined and applied to so many of the hawk family. Like the sharp-shin, it is a bold, flashy hunter, and having a continent-wide range it has afforded many farmers the opportunity of seeing it in action around the hen house! Being an accipiter, it has the maneuverable long tail and powerful rounded wings designed for acceleration—a combination very efficient.

This hawk prefers softwood trees for nesting and, though it occasionally uses hardwoods, the nests will usually be found built against the trunk of a pine tree. It is a well-woven, flat nest of sticks lined with inner barks, chips, pine sprigs, and a few weeds. It will use nests of other species and redecorate them but prefers to build new ones each year. Three to five young are raised.

The long, barred tail often sticks out over the nest, making the inhabitant's identity known. The tail is rounded and is used to great advantage in steering as this bird bursts through the woods in its quest for food—partridge, squirrels, rabbits, smaller hawks, birds in general, *anything!*

Like the sharp-shin, this hawk is basically gray above, light and barred beneath. The females are browner above. As adults they have the traditional accipiter red eye, and can attain a length of over twenty inches.

SHARP-SHINNED HAWK (*Accipiter striatus*)

Similar in shape and coloration to the Cooper's hawk, this fellow differs in size, being a good bit smaller, and his tail is squared-off instead of rounded. A large female sharp-shin might be about the same size as a small male Cooper's hawk—about fourteen inches long.

This bird prefers pine, cedar, spruce, or hemlock for its nest, and will generally choose a tree near the edge of a clearing. Built at varying heights, the nests are usually shallow, located on a horizontal limb near the trunk. Some are lined with grasses, leaves, and green sprigs, while others have nothing but a finer weave of small twigs in the lining. Widely distributed, these birds can be found over the whole of North and Central America.

These hawks are primarily bird eaters, taking anything in size from a dove to a nuthatch. They have been known to attack birds far larger, even a night heron! Rodents are taken as well as insects of various sorts. They are swift and crafty hunters, often pouncing upon their prey before it realizes the danger.

Bold, reckless, audacious—just some of the words used to describe the sharp-shin. This hawk has been observed stealing a retrieved bird from under a dog's nose, chasing a bird into a house, and another through a chicken-wire fence. My friend Cecil would call it "some old rugged!"

124

OSPREY (*Pandion haliaetus*)

This widely distributed bird resembles in some respects falcons, accipiters, eagles, and vultures, so it has been put into a category of its own. It has a very small head for the size of its beak, and has owl-like toes—two forward and two behind. The bottom of the feet are covered with spicules for a sandpapery grip, and large, curved, equally sized talons further that ability. The wings are long and slender with a noticeable angle to them, reaching a spread of up to six feet. When sitting this large brown and white bird is rather ungainly, but when soaring or diving for food its grace is unsurpassed.

The osprey takes fish from the surface after a long treetop vigil or a flight over the water. It will also hover up to a hundred fifty feet above the surface, then fall in a falconlike stoop, often disappearing beneath the waves. The prey is then carried head first to the nest or eaten on a convenient perch.

Osprey nests have been built on cliffs, mud bogs, trees, navigation markers, telephone poles, all manner of sites—just so long as they are near water and fish. Some of the sites are low enough to fall prey to various predators, and humans as well. The nests are large, up to four feet across, and can become very deep as they are added to year after year. In addition to sticks, the osprey will add many other materials. Nests investigated have included kelp, laths, shingles, parts of life preservers, pieces of netting, cork, rope, sponges, a toy boat, conch eggs, a broom, a feather duster, rubber boots, ad infinitum. Incredible!

Osprey generally raise two young. Due to pesticide use and its retention by fish, the large osprey colonies have declined rapidly since the forties. It was twenty-five years ago that this decline in population was first noticed. Now, due to the banning of DDT, there seems to be an indication that in some areas this bird is becoming more stable. A worldwide citizen, this bird is absent only in the Antarctic.

MARSH HAWK (*Circus cyaneus*)

This bird chooses marshes, fields, and plains across our continent—any open country where its prey may dwell to make its rounds in its quest for food. Whether marsh or hilltop, the chief prey is the mouse—meadow, field, vole, or others. While the female incubates the eggs, the male hunts. He returns to drop the meal to the female either on the nest or in midair. If the latter, she flies up and snatches it as it falls. The nest is built on the ground, usually well hidden in reeds or grasses. The male brings suitable material to his mate and she then constructs the nest from straw, weeds, grasses, and small sticks, till a suitable thickness is attained, usually two to fifteen inches. The thicker nests are constructed on wetter ground. Four to six eggs are laid, both parents share the incubation, and when the young are developed enough to tear their own food, both parents range far afield. They drop the prey into the nest and continue on their hunt. The main fare is mice, but they also take partridge, water birds such as small ducks and bitterns, and various amphibians. Often thought of as devoted homebodies, they nevertheless are aggressive and competent hunters, and are protective of their nest sites. In addition to nesting on the ground these hawks roost on the ground as well—a dangerous habit, I should think.

This hawk reaches a length of over one and a half feet. The males are gray above and the females brown.

GOSHAWK (*Accipiter gentilis*)

This is the largest, boldest, and fiercest of our North American accipiters. I think it is probably the fiercest creature with wings. Like the sharp-shinned and Cooper's hawks, it is a marvel of maneuverability, its thick, blunt wings and long tail providing the tools needed for rapid, twisting flight through dense woods. It hunts fast and low, requiring but a flick of its tail to counterfeint and fasten ferociously to its prey. Much poultry has succumbed to the goshawk. One incident related in Bent's *Life Histories of Birds of Prey* by a Mr. Farley in Maine:

> *A goshawk caught a half-grown hen. The hen, escaping, ran under a woman's skirts. The hawk followed right up to the skirt but was killed. They had to kill the hen, too, for its crop was torn open as a result of the hawk's fierce grip.*

This and other such stories attest to the hawk's boldness. The goshawk builds a large and close-knit nest; one was reported to be five feet across, though three feet would be more normal.

The site is usually in dense woods far from possible intrusion. Canada and the far northern states are this bird's general range, but now and again one will be found as far south as Pennsylvania. It prefers no particular variety of tree, but more often than not will choose the tallest one in the vicinity, nesting up to seventy feet high. Three to five eggs are laid.

There have been many species of birds and mammals recorded as prey for the goshawk. Suffice it to say that it will eat whatever it can overpower, and that takes in a lot of territory: anything up to and including the size of a woodchuck.

The adult goshawk is gray on the top with a dark cap and white streak over the eye; the female is browner on top. Its tail is very long and barred black. The bird grows to two feet long and has a four-foot wing span. If you ever get close enough to see it, the eye is quite red in adults.

GYRFALCON (*Falco rusticolus*)

The gyrfalcon is the largest of the family Falconidae. It is not only larger, with a body which may be over two feet, but more heavily built as well. One thinks of a gyrfalcon as a white bird with a few black markings, but it ranges from white to nearly black and encompasses all the shades between. The different shades can be found within one group of nestlings. The female gyrfalcon is similar in color to the male, but is much larger, and in some cases twice the weight. In the smaller falcons color differences tend to mark the sexes, and though size differences are supposed to be a giveaway, it is often hard to tell those at a glance.

Living in the northernmost reaches of Europe, Asia, and the Americas, this bird is a resident of the open tundra, a bleak and inhospitable area offering little cover to its prey. Long chases have made the gyrfalcon the champion endurance flyer of its group. The peregrine on the other hand, must strike suddenly, as in most of its territory there is ample opportunity for its prey to escape, to hide in woods or thickets.

Gyrfalcon nesting is accomplished on a ledge or outcropping, and the nests found indicate they have been used for years. They are heaped with droppings, sticks, bones, and the remains of many meals. Not tidy housekeepers! They feed primarily on ptarmigans, filling in with ducks, hares, lemmings, shore birds, and sea birds.

The gyrfalcon was prized and used for hunting by royalty—I've mentioned the class distinction in falconry—and I've often wondered what the penalty was if a serf was caught using a peregrine or gyrfalcon.

125

SPARROW HAWK (*Falco sparverius*)

This, the smallest of the falcons, is a familiar sight to anyone in America who has driven many country miles. It is commonly seen perching on telephone wires, surveying fields or roadsides for an adventuresome mouse. When landing in trees, it most often chooses the very tip, balancing precariously where no toehold seems possible.

One identifying characteristic of this bird is its habit of hovering in place, wings beating rapidly, as it surveys a mousy spot in a field.

Mice form the largest part of the diet, with all manner of insects filling in. When hunting is difficult or demand high, as when the bird has a nest full of young, these hawks will add small birds to the larder.

A hole in a tree, often an old woodpecker's nest, a natural cavity, or even a nesting box serves well as a nesting site. I put out seven boxes on my old farm, and all were occupied by hawks, some only after I evicted wintered-over pairs of flying squirrels! These birds will nest in buildings as well, provided the nesting interior is sealed from view or intrusion.

Four or five white eggs are deposited and hatched after twenty-eight to thirty days of incubation. I noticed at our nests the incubating female would emerge in the middle of the afternoon, responding to a shrill call by the male. While she remained away from the nest, usually about half an hour, the male incubated. Unlike most birds, the sparrow hawk adds no nesting material, using whatever chips or leftovers happen to remain in the site. I suppose there are exceptions, but I haven't found any. The pair will return year after year to the same nest.

The female is brown above and light below. The male has a gray cap and blue-gray wings.

Long favored by beginning falconers, these gentle birds continue to be numerous.

PRAIRIE FALCON (*Falco mexicanus*)

This bird's territory covers the western half of the United States and reaches into Canada. True to the name, it does indeed frequent the open prairie areas where the absence of obstructions permits the all-out speed for which the falcons are so famous. At least in the open we have more opportunities to see them at work. They inhabit foothills and mountains as well, and are adept at securing food no matter what the terrain.

The choice of prey runs the gamut from ground squirrels, other rodent species, quail, partridge, ducks, doves, and myriad smaller birds such as sparrows, blackbirds, or whatever happens by at the right time.

The prairie falcon is similar in size to the peregrine, and their territories overlap considerably. They select similar nesting sites, usually high in a rocky outcropping or cliff, sheltered by an overhang or in a crevice. There is little if any nesting material. The prairie falcon's eggs are lighter in color than the peregrine's, being white or buff covered with various splotches, spots, and dots. There are three to five eggs. This hawk will also nest on the ground if ideal sites are not available.

The prairie falcon looks much like the peregrine, but without the dark helmet. It has a moustache stripe and is usually somewhat sandy in color, although it, like other birds, has light and dark phases. The head markings are the quickest way to tell the difference between the two birds.

I have a friend who is a falconer and has a bird that is a cross between a peregrine and a prairie falcon. It looks at first glance to be a peregrine, but a bit more pale. It was not a natural cross, but a product of artificial insemination.

BROAD-WINGED HAWK (*Buteo platypterus*)

This hawk can often be seen anywhere in the eastern half of our country, soaring high, circling, and searching for its next meal—a meal of mouse, snake, frog, bird, insects of every description, and even toads. The broad-wing appears to be a rather retiring and quiet hawk except during mating, when he and his mate call and cavort about the sky in a seemingly recreational manner. It is a gentle bird, a bird of the woods. It has been reported that when brooding, one broad-wing allowed an observer to remove it from the nest. This bird seems to have no preference in types of trees used for nesting. It nests infrequently in old hawk or squirrel nests, but more often builds a nest of loose sticks, lined with bark chips and a few green sprigs. The nest is next to the trunk and two or three eggs are laid. The young are fed by the parents, who strip small morsels from the prey.

This hawk is brown above, light underneath with lightbrown barring which becomes heavier and almost solid at the sides of the throat. A female I once measured was eighteen inches long.

In the fall over our old farm in the Delaware Valley, we used to see thousands of broad-wings streaming south over a period of several days.

RED-SHOULDERED HAWK (*Buteo lineatus*)

These hawks range the eastern half of the United States, though they appear to be increasingly rare. They inhabit lowland woods, building large nests in a main tree crotch. The nest, though large and heavily built, is carefully lined with greenery, moss, lichens, leaves, and down from the bird's breast.

They hatch three to five young to whom they feed all manner of rodents, insects, birds, and reptiles. As the youngsters grow, their adventurous nature takes over and they venture farther and farther out onto limbs of the home tree, returning to the nest at night. Their first flights are clumsy affairs, but before long they learn their parents' technique of gliding swiftly through the woods, as agile there among hundreds of obstructions as a gyrfalcon over the open tundra.

This hawk tends to intercept the nest observer with much commotion, and many attacks have been recorded. In spite of intrusions the red-shouldered hawk sticks to its home woods, continuing to rebuild or use nests from previous years. It is a large hawk, reaching two feet in length.

EVERGLADES KITE (*Rostrhamus sociabilis*)

The marshes and swampy areas that were so abundant in Florida till the 1930s were the habitat for this bird's food, the snail. When real estate operators and engineers began improving the state "for the good of Man" by draining large areas to make them more valuable for building and agriculture, they disregarded the effect upon wildlife. Money talks, and the kites were among those who didn't have enough to fight back with. The snails died off, surviving in only those few small areas of the Everglades that are wet year round, and the kites declined in proportion.

The male is a slate gray bird with a white tip and base on his tail feathers, and has red skin around his eyes and beak. The female is mottled brown, and has a white eyebrow quite like the goshawk's. The beak of the kite is long and slim, especially suited for extracting the snail's body from its shell.

Nests are built low in palmettos or reeds three to ten feet high and are made of small twigs and leaves. They are twelve to sixteen inches across, six to ten inches deep, and are not very carefully constructed. Two to four eggs are laid. They have a white ground color and vary so in spottiness and blotching colors that it would be silly to try to describe one as typical.

The kite survives in some abundance in Central and South America, especially in Brazil where vast areas of wetlands still exist.

126

HARRIS' HAWK (*Parabuteo unicinctus*)

To me this is one of the most beautiful of the hawks. Most of the plumage is so dark brown it appears almost black, and the shoulders are accented by reddish-brown feathers. The tail is tipped with white, and the upper coverts are white as well. Clear, slatey-colored skin and beak are set off by a pale yellow nostril area (*cere*).

An aquaintance of mine had a Harris' trained for hunting, so I got a good closeup. It is a large hawk, reaching two feet long, and as such has a great variety of prey species it can dominate. Wood rats are a large percentage of the diet. Ground squirrels, snakes, rabbits, herons, ducks—again, whatever it can overpower will do. These hawks have been observed pursuing quarry into dense cover just as an accipiter might do; consequently, they have the aggressiveness sought in a good, trained bird.

The nest site of the Harris' hawk depends on the bird's territory. In the desert a mesquite or yucca, or perhaps a large, branched cactus, will be chosen. On the plains any tree will do—cottonwood, elm, anything, just to get the nest up in the air. The eggs are usually white with sometimes very faint buff markings, and three or four are laid.

This hawk ranges from our Southwest through Central America, all the way to the southern tip of South America.

SWAINSON'S HAWK (*Buteo swainsoni*)

These birds may be seen throughout the western half of the United States, though they are best known in the plains states. They appear in the spring in flocks ranging from ten to hundreds in number. They eat a variety of items, and other birds are rarely among them. Mice and insects form the largest part of their diet. Reports of large numbers of Swainson's hawks patrolling fields on foot searching for and devouring grasshoppers and crickets have been repeated year after year. These hawks will use a fence post as a hunting perch, sometimes sitting for hours till a luckless mouse ventures forth. They also pay strict attention to a farmer who may be driving a piece of equipment in a field, consequently flushing forth an occasional mouse. I have seen foxes following a tractor and plow for the same reason.

Swainson's nests are in trees, either evergreen or deciduous, and on rock outcroppings. Some are at staggering heights, and some are within arm's reach. The nests are constructed quite like the red-tailed hawk's, large, stick affairs lined with softer materials in which are laid two to four pale blue green eggs, the surfaces of which are sprinkled with splotches of various browns.

This bird is various shades of browns with light underparts. For me the best way to identify it is by the dark bib it seems to have on the upper part of the chest.

FERRUGINOUS ROUGH-LEGGED HAWK (*Buteo regalis*)

This is a large bird, exceeding two feet in length, with light underparts and no markings on the tails of the adults. A relative, the rough-legged hawk of the far north, does have a heavy tail band.

Prairie dogs, mice, gophers, and other rodents are pursued by these hawks with great success. They may hunt from a perch, on the wing low to the ground or high, and even standing on the ground itself, waiting for the unwary to surface, thinking the way is clear. An extremely patient bird, the ferruginous is a most successful hunter.

Nests are big, made from large sticks built in a tree or rocky area at whatever height suits: sometimes six feet, sometimes a hundred. They try to build them where they will have a commanding view of the surrounding countryside. Sticks up to one inch thick are used and the nests will be lined with soft grasses, rootlets, and leaves. In eastern Washington a man named J. H. Bowles discovered a nest "as large as a very large eagle nest," and added that "it took up almost the entire tree." An accumulation of years and years of redecorating. One large nest had within its substructure the nest of a magpie, complete with eggs!

Two to five eggs are laid; they have a light background with light brown splotches covered with darker brown splotches on top.

PIGEON HAWK (*Falco columbarius*)

A pair of pigeon hawks nests on Loud's island each year and may be seen near their favorite hunting field several times a week, all summer long. They hunt the whole field but are most active along the great walls of spruce that border it. They often sit hidden in the thickly needled branches, waiting for a foolish bird to show itself within their territory, or a juicy grasshopper to flush forth from its cover.

The food list for this bird is immense. Plovers, snipe, woodcock, sandpipers, quail, doves, and hundreds of smaller birds find their way into this hawk's crop. Squirrels, mice, frogs, snakes, grasshoppers, every manner of bug—really, just everything is fair game. Unlike the larger falcons, who hunt from a great altitude, these small hawks rely more on stealth and a mad dash to obtain food. Naturally more aggressive than some hawks, these birds are even reported to have entered pigeon boxes and stolen prize domestic birds. I think these may be somewhat overblown, for the hawks are about the same size as a pigeon, and I doubt if they could handle the weight in flight. Maybe.

They seem to prefer a spruce or a pine tree for nesting, but others are used. A stick nest, usually well protected by surrounding foliage and well lined with soft materials, is built to hold the three to five heavily blotched eggs. The nest of another bird, if in suitable cover, is sometimes relined and used. Tree cavities, sheltered spots in rocky outcrops, and even ground sites have been observed. On Loud's, the choice is a spruce tree.

These birds are a tad longer than a sparrow hawk. The male has a gray head cap, gray upper parts, and is light underneath with brown streaks. The female is your basic brown on top and streaky below. They both have broadly banded tails.